To L...

from

Hugh Cameron

Jan 2020

HAVE KNIFE,
WILL TRAVEL

HAVE KNIFE,
WILL TRAVEL

Hugh Cameron

Rev. date: 08/16/2019

To order additional copies of this book, contact:
Xlibris
1-888-795-4274
www.Xlibris.com
Orders@Xlibris.com
800882

CONTENTS

The author is Dr. Hugh Cameron, a world-famous orthopedic surgeon, who for years was at the forefront of the development of artificial joints. He is a professor in surgery with previous cross appointments also in pathology, bioengineering, and graduate studies at the University of Toronto. He was an adjunct professor of engineering at the University of Waterloo. He has published more than two hundred scientific articles and two technical books, one entitled *The Technique of Total Hip Replacement*. This is the story of the development of these artificial joints and how he and a band of brothers crisscrossed the world, teaching this new technology to thousands of other surgeons to the benefit of millions of patients who now walk pain-free as a result.

It is a lighthearted view of the trials, tribulations, and fun in the development and introduction of world-changing technology.

INTRODUCTION

Artificial joint replacement was one of the miracles of modern medicine. New knees and hips had allowed thousands upon thousands of people to live happy and productive lives; whereas, previously they would have been destined to become cripples, largely confined at home and excluded from work and society.

This book is a lighthearted look at the coming of age of one of the pioneers of joint replacement surgery. It briefly examines the boyhood, education, and training, which set the scene for discoveries that were made to enable patients to be offered new joints, which would potentially function well as their own and last them for the rest of their lives.

After attending medical school in St. Andrews in Scotland, the author did his specialist training in Toronto, at that time a hub of frenetic research activity. There was the palpable excitement of the '70s, bursting with new concepts, ideas, and new ways of looking at the world. It was a can-do time in the world's history, when men were on the moon and there was every prospect of new colonies being established on the high frontier of space. There was a feeling that nothing was impossible.

Everything was in a state of flux. There was supersonic air transportation. Undersea habitats were being explored. The monster Stalin was long dead, and Khrushchev, hammering his shoe on the desk at the UN, threatening mayhem, was exiting stage left. Youth felt it was taking over, with slogans like "Trust no one over age thirty." The birth control pill was now in general use, which radically changed the behavior of the young.

As part of this strange and exhilarating world, the radical technique of fixing implants to bones by inducing the bone to grow into the implant was being explored by an engineer, Bob Pilliar, and the author. As this was completely new, a vast amount of research was required before it could be released for use on humans. Within a decade, it became the preferred method of implant fixation in use worldwide. This method, now in use for more than four decades, had proved durable, and implants could now be fixed to bones permanently, no matter how much they were loaded. Patients had gone from walking cautiously with a cane to playing tennis and downhill skiing.

As well as solving the fixation problem, there were also the design issues of the artificial joints. Simply making a copy of the natural human joint was not practical, so various design, mechanical, and material issues had to be worked out. Knee and hip replacements are now so good that patients are being told to expect twenty-five or thirty years out of a joint before it wears out, and when it does, the bearings can be changed like the brakes on a car. It is not necessary to change the whole car.

Because this was completely new, the surgeons who would have to insert these things had to be taught. Prior to this disruptive technology, teaching of medicine really had not changed for eons. It was done via universities, which was a slow and incomplete method of doing so. Pioneered by the Swiss trauma surgeons, a new way of teaching was introduced, and surgeon designers, funded by the companies who made the implants, set out around the world to teach these new concepts and new techniques.

There were about five major companies and about twenty surgeons involved in what became known as the Traveling Road Show. For more than twenty years, these surgeons crisscrossed the world, teaching joint replacement surgery, as the increasing wealth worldwide meant that more countries became able to afford this type of surgery.

The education and training of a surgeon is outlined, along with the lives, loves, thrills, and spills of the operating room, which for a surgeon is the real world. What happens outside is somewhat peripheral. The intricate dance of the surgeon and the OR nurses is described, and the change in cultural mores from the freewheeling seventies, which were introduced by the Pill, and headlined by Woodstock in 1969. The customs, interactions, and episodes are almost unimaginable in the current return to the puritanical age of the last decade or so.

The world continues to evolve, and the internet and the electronic age make it unlikely that the introduction of similar disruptive technology will require such hands-on physical teaching. Printing of organs is not far away, and if the problem of AI being able to recognize and filter reality is solved, then surgery will become similar to video games. The Traveling Road Show is already vanishing into history, and the surgeon will soon become an interesting relic, like the stonemasons of the medieval cathedrals.

SUGGESTED FRONTISPIECE
Postrerini 1138612815

CHAPTER 1

THE BEGINNING

The first thing I remember is looking up at an operating room light.

I was a little boy. I had contracted tuberculosis from the milk of an infected cow. Fortunately, it was in the neck glands only, and the surgeon in the local town elected to simply aspirate the abscess. He did this I don't know how many times, but it eventually healed. There was no anesthetic, and I don't remember anyone holding me down, although maybe they did. I remember the nurses laughing because I would wriggle my feet while not moving anything else. My father would buy me a bottle of American cream soda pop after the procedure. I never saw that drink in America, but it was hugely popular in Scotland.

I grew up in a mining village in the center of Scotland called Slamannan. There must have been miners who came back from North America because there were tiny groups of houses a few miles from the village named after the places from the Gold Rush era, such as a collection of three houses called Dawson City and another group called California. Why anyone would come back to that godforsaken place in the Scottish moors, I never understood, even as a child.

It was called a mining village because that was all there was. There was one small brick manufacturing works, mining, and military. The surrounding farms were pretty much subsistence. The land was poor, boggy, and filled with steep little hills. These were so steep that it was unsafe to use tractors to plow as they would roll over. Most farmers had plough horse. I remember these as being a gigantic breed called Clydesdales. Sitting on the back of one of these horses was like sitting with your legs open on a kitchen table.

The men who went off to join the military were treated with respect. This, after all, had been a common occupation in Scotland for centuries. The tales of the Scottish mercenaries were frequently told to children, like the story of Sandy Leckie. Oliver Cromwell had been having some trouble in Scotland, so he simply hired Sandy Leckie, who was Scottish, but was one of Frederick the Great's generals. Sandy came over from Germany, reorganized the English army, whipped the Scots, and went back to Germany.

As you can see, we had somewhat mixed loyalties in the village. Our one true hero was Sandy Binnie. In the First World War, Sandy was in the trenches. A British soldier was wounded and caught on the barbed wire in the middle of no-man's-land. He was screaming and crying all night, and of course, no one could get to him. Sandy listened to him for a long time and could not stand it any longer. He crawled out of his trench and across the mud to rescue the man. He had just cut the man off the wire and put him on his back to carry him back to his trench when the Germans put up a star shell.

As Sandy would say, there he was standing in the middle of no-man's-land with a man on his back, and it was bright as day. The machine guns opened up. They had tracer rounds in them, so Sandy could watch the streams of bullets converging on him, and there was nothing he could do. Just before the stream of bullets reached him, a German officer jumped up on the parapet of his trench, waved his arms, and shouted *nien*. The machine guns stopped, and Sandy carried the man back to his own trench under the light of the star shell. He got the Military Medal for that feat of valor.

One of the great stories I remember was written by Neil Munro. A group of Scottish mercenaries were sitting around talking. One of them, John Splendid, was speaking, "Heart of a rose, *Gra mo chroi*, bird song at the lip, star eye, and wisdom, yet woman to the core. I wish I were as young as I then was, but *Ochanee*, what would avail my teens if the one woman that ever understood me were but dust in Golgo. She died a stainless maid in Golgo, in Silesia. Hoots, toots, here I am on an old man's story. In times of leisure, I cheat myself into the notion that once I loved a foreign lass who died a stainless maid."

It must have been sixty years or more since I first read that, and it is as moving to me today as it was then.

The mines around the village were awful, a vision of hell. The coal seams were narrow, so the men worked in a squatting position with a pick and shovel. Many were below the water table, so the men might have their backside in water as they squatted. It was a true Orwellian nightmare. Sometimes they would break through a wall, and the water would come in and drown them like rats in a trap.

The squatting and torquing position meant that they would frequently tear the medial meniscus in their knee. This was so common among miners in Scotland that my old professor, Ian Smillie, became world-famous for developing knives to remove a torn meniscus. I used these knives in my first year of residency in the seventies. If a meniscus is removed, it is like removing the oiling pad from a bearing. Twenty or thirty years later, the bearing wears out, and the patient needs a knee replacement; only there were no knee replacements in those days. As everyone smoked and all the miners had black lung, I doubt many lived to the age when they would have needed it in any case.

I still remember working on one medical ward in Scotland. The consultant said that he probably could not teach us medical students much other than to know when to let someone go. I have the feeling, which may not be correct, that if a patient was older than sixty-five, they were told to go away and sit in the corner and stop bothering people. I vividly remember my first case in Canada. It was an old lady who had broken her hip. The senior resident operated on her. She died the next day as about 20 percent did then. The family asked me what had happened. I explained to them that she was ninety-five and she died. I mean, that happens to ninety-five-year-olds. The family was extremely upset.

"She came in here a fit, healthy ninety-five-year-old, and now she's dead."

I did not understand what the fuss was about, and it took my chief some time to settle down the family. It certainly was a different way of looking at the world.

The boys I went to primary school with went down the mines at sixteen. At eighteen, they were married, and at twenty, they had children. These were men. I look around today, and I don't know what to say about the thirty-year-olds living in their mother's basement. My father had been a miner. The pit boss told him he was too intelligent to do that and encouraged him to sit an examination. From the pit face, he got a scholarship to Glasgow University and became a Presbyterian minister. Having been a miner and seen the appalling circumstances they lived in, he was a lifelong socialist.

I remember when strip mining came in. They would simply tear the top of a mountain and strip out the coal. The proto-environmentalists of that day objected bitterly to the mess, but my father looked on with satisfaction. He said that he was pleased that men would never again have to go under the ground like moles.

Every summer, I remember the terror of polio. It is hard to convey to anyone nowadays the awful sense of doom that every summer would bring. One boy in my class, who must have been age six, got polio and was left with a paralyzed leg and a double-sided iron brace for the rest of his life. My parents would not let my brothers and me near the village children the whole summer. The world let out an incredible sigh of relief when the Salk injectable polio immunization first came out, followed shortly by the Sabin oral. And now I hear of people not immunizing their children because of some junk science, which were lies to begin with and had long since been disproved and withdrawn. Oh well, sic transit gloria mundi.

CHAPTER 2

THE VILLAGE

A mining village was a tough place. The boys settled arguments with fistfights, and the adults stayed away. The fight was over when someone would not get up again. I don't remember any serious injuries, as it was bare-knuckle. The men also settled things with their fists. I doubt that my village was any different than any other village, but I do remember many interesting stories. A violent place tended to be a polite place, unless one was deliberately looking for mayhem.

* * *

Polly owned the only fish-and-chips shop. She was from the village and had made her money in London during the Second World War. She had been what is euphemistically called a working girl. She had retired and returned to the village and would come to my father's church every Sunday in her nice suit and big hat. My father liked her very much and called her Mary Magdalene. He said she did it more for love than for money, giving these young soldiers the comfort of her own body before they went off to fight and die.

One night, a visitor to the village called Polly a whore. Technically, I suppose he was correct, but that was in the past, and he had insulted Polly. An insult like that needed an answer. Someone went to Polly's half brother, Ian.

He was a mild, inoffensive little man, who had never had a fight in his life. But this was Scotland, and Polly was his half sister, and honor must be satisfied. So Ian put on his boots and went up the street to do battle. He knocked the man down, and normally, that would be the end of it. But a woman had been insulted, so Ian "put the boot in," as we used to say in Scotland. I do remember being told the man eventually made a sort of recovery.

*   *   *

There was the story of Big John Smiley. There was a terrible family in the village. They were a large clan of fighting Irish. The Scots were the Red Celts, and the Irish, the Black Celts, so of course, they hated each other. That was a long time ago, and I don't know if that is still the case. The rumor is, or was, that the Irish are the Black Celts because of the number of Spanish soldiers who washed up on the beaches of Ireland after the disaster of the Spanish Armada.

One evening, on the bus coming back from the local town, one of the Irish families was drunk and giving the bus conductress a hard time. Big John sat down beside him and held him down until they got back to the village. A short time later, Big John was sitting at his supper when his front windows shattered, and there was the Irishman on the front lawn, stripped to the waist, swinging an axe.

Big John, who was afraid of nothing on God's earth, went out the front door. His son, Little John, went out the back door. By the time the boy came around the side of the house, Big John had grappled with the man, but the man had cut him with the axe. The boy saw his father's blood. He picked up a two-by-four and hit his father's assailant so hard on the head that the man had difficulty remembering his name thereafter.

*   *   *

There were many other stories, like that of the man who went missing. A man went missing. The rumor was that he had been seeing someone else's wife. The husband found out. The man came calling when the husband was supposed to be at work. A window had been left open. The man unwisely put his head in through the open window. Rumor had it that a garden spade was waiting for him and that he and his head were buried in a bog out on the moors.

There was also the story of the Tiger. One night, a carload of drunk people hit an old man on his bicycle. They did not stop. The old man was unconscious, headed down on a steep hill. The coroner said he drowned in his own blood. The village knew who did it, but there was no proof. That Sunday, a young boy turned up in my father's church with the family Bible. They still had family Bibles in those days. The boy was the only male relative of the old man in the village. The only other male member of the family was a man called the Tiger, who had left to join the merchant marine ten or more years before.

The family sent for the Tiger. It took two years to find him, as he was on the South American run. The devil, in this case, is in the name. People called Rhino or Tiger in the merchant marine are to be avoided at all costs. It was not good to annoy a man with a name like that. The Tiger came home. He had been away so long no one recognized him. He went to the local pub and picked a fight with the man the family was certain was responsible. They went up to the village bowling green to settle the issue. The Tiger was taking off his shirt when the man attacked him, head down. The coroner said later that the man had a thin skull. Maybe, but in the forty years of medical practice, I still have never heard of one man breaking another man's head with his fists.

The local policeman, who was no one's fool, charged the Tiger with murder. The crowd who had witnessed the fight and the legal charges came to see my father for advice. In the local town, there were two well-known lawyers: one you went to if you were innocent and one if you were guilty. My father phoned the guilty lawyer, who proved as good as his reputation. The procurator fiscal, who is the Scottish equivalent to the DA—as Scottish law is Roman law, not English common law—tried to get the charges reduced to manslaughter. If he had done that, then the Tiger would be jailed for ten years. The Tiger's lawyer refused, so the Tiger stood trial for murder. No Scottish jury, hearing a story like that, was going to convict, so the Tiger walked free. I actually knew the Tiger. I never saw him raise his voice. Maybe he did not need to. He was not a tall man, but he had very broad shoulders and huge hands.

In spite of the odd confrontations—such as Matt Wotherspoon with a garden spade and a couple of Irishmen with wooden clubs, a high-noon-type meeting—the village was a relatively peaceful place, as mining villages go. I certainly liked it. My father was given shooting rights over the local landowner's property, and my father's gravedigger taught me to shoot. Shotguns were the only weapons allowed in Britain unless there were special circumstances. My father had an old 1912 US long-barrel gun, which I used initially.

The gravedigger was an elegant little man. He taught me not only shooting but also other tricks, such as snaring rabbits and even pheasants, if you could identify their runs. He taught me the technique of long-lining the river, which is absolutely illegal. One buys about thirty feet of clothesline and attach droppers with worms on a hook every six feet or so. This device is tied to a stake hammered into the bank and thrown into the river, after the water bailiff has gone to bed. One then gets up at 6:00 a.m., before the water bailiff gets up and pulls in the line, which usually has a couple of trout attached to it. He justified this thievery by explaining that we were cleaning the big cannibal trout out of the river. I liked him very much. When I left to go to university, he gave me his prized, beautifully chased, double-barrel shotgun.

I had fun with that shotgun at university. The boy I was sharing a room with in residency was from the south of England, and he and his brother were really good shots. We used to go down to the estuary of the River Tay and lie in the mud, waiting for the dawn flight to come over. The brother, who was a postgraduate in marine biology, had a place where he could cook them. We were fairly well-known as shooters, so one day, some young ladies proposed having a barbecue on the beach and asked us to shoot something for them. This was the socialite group as St. Andrews was a party university, and none of us really knew them, as we were only poor working-class stiffs. We went out therefore and slaughtered the seagulls. We skinned them and parboiled them to get rid of the worst of the scum and told the young ladies they were partridges. We ate nothing at that barbecue. The old Scottish name for a seagull is a shit hawk. If one ever wishes to see where the town sewer opens into the sea, that is where there is a flock of seagulls.

I also had a folding shotgun. I don't remember where I got it, but I used it for poaching. A folding gun folds up and can be placed inside one's pant leg. You have to walk with a stiff knee, but that is better than trying to run away. When I was doing a fellowship in London, I once went north with my old friend Peter Aston to watch a car rally through the woods. During that race, I was standing at the crown of a double right-hand bend. I could hear the engine bellowing as the first car was coming up the hill. As he came over the crown of the hill, the driver put his front wheels on full left lock and skidded his rear end through the double right-hand corner without taking his foot off the accelerator. It was unbelievably skillful.

On that trip, I met Frank from Nottingham. He worked for Rolls-Royce, making aircraft engines. Frank had many stories to tell, like the time they wished to check the engine for bird strike. Visiting dignitaries were standing around to watch. Some jackass went and got a frozen chicken from the supermarket and, still frozen, threw it into the jet engine while it was firing in its test bed. There was a loud explosion, and the air was full of bits and pieces of the engine, including several stator wheels, which almost decapitated the visitors.

Frank rebuilds old Triumph sports cars for fun, as he could make the parts himself. He also built a crossbow from Titanium for hunting, as it was silent. It was so powerful he could put a bolt through a tree. I had supper at Frank's place once. The venison and the pheasant were excellent. Frank made all sorts of instruments for me for hip replacement surgery while I was in London. When I went back to Canada, I left my folding shotgun with him.

The land attached to the manse, or church house, where I lived in had forty acres, so there was plenty of space. Neither I nor my brothers were ever interested in team sports. Probably the village was too small for any teams, but we were interested in track and field. We had endless books from the local library about Paavo Nurmi and the flying Finns and other noted athletes. For some reason, which escapes me, I was Da Silva, the Brazilian long jumper. We built long-jump pits, high-jump pits, etc. My elder brother was a pretty good middle-distance runner, so a coach came up from one of the local towns and marked out a two-hundred-meter running track.

In his running school, this coach had a boy who won the Scottish junior cross-country and Mick Ryan, who later immigrated to New Zealand, and got bronze in the Commonwealth Games Steeplechase. My brother got an athletic scholarship to a university in California. I never had the ability to push myself like that. One could hear stories of some of the great Tour de France riders. One was quoted as having said, "Legs, shut up!" Nonetheless, I remember doing repetitive two-hundred-meter sprints until the vomit comes, then you run some more repetitions. "Give each child a trophy" this was not. We used to do a Swedish thing called fartlek; it was simply running over rough country for two or three hours.

CHAPTER 3

THE WORLD OF SPORTS

What I liked was the shot put. I did it in the front yard. Many of my father's visitors would pick up the shot, which weighed about twelve pounds, and heave it. My hero was the American Parry O'Brien. At age twelve, I got weights and became the strong boy. I was big for my age but, unfortunately, stopped growing shortly thereafter. My high school gym teacher was a great man. This could never happen nowadays. At lunchtime, he would allow about half a dozen boys into the gym. There were no restrictions. We had a trampoline, climbing rails, and weights. Do what you want. There was no supervision. He was very strict about who could come in—only a very few kids who were very well coordinated. I remember doing crazy things, but no one ever got hurt. No school in North America would ever allow that now. The insurance would be impossibly high.

Not that supervision necessarily did any good if there was no common sense. I was involved in a tragic legal case in Canada, not as a doctor, but because I did some work at a very good engineering school, supervising the student's theses. One of my engineering friends was asked to consult on a very bad case. A kid, who was heavy and not well coordinated, was asked to use the rings by his gym teacher. Rings are difficult for anyone who is not a gymnast, and certainly, no boy who does not have outstanding coordination should ever be on the rings. This poor kid fell off and broke his neck, resulting in permanent paralysis.

For some reason, I forgot why we had to show that if the padding under the rings had been thicker, he might not have broken his neck. We bought a crash dummy from General Motors, who used them to simulate crashes, so they had instrumented the neck of the dummy with accelerometers and other measuring devices. As an aside, that being the case, I have never understood why no car company in the world has ever made a decent car seat. They are all designed for Schumacher, sitting straight back, with his head and body strapped to the seat. I was operating in Italy once near Maranello, and I actually got the opportunity to sit in the Ferrari that Schumacher had won the Formula One title the year before.

The only decent car seat I ever sat on was in the Vega, America's worst car. Everyone sits in a car with the spine curved into a C-shape. No one sits straight. This means that when the headrest was pulled up, it should come forward as well as up, not back, dummies! Anyway, I am pleased to recall that the kid with the broken neck got a very large settlement, but I don't think anyone would trade dollars for paralysis. I never ceased to blame the teacher. That boy should never have been on the rings.

My high school gym teacher in Scotland was cleaning out his back room one day when he found an old throwing hammer he did not know was there. He had no use for it, so he gave it to me. I took it home. My father found a Polish man, George Kordas, in a nearby town, who knew how to throw the thing. In Scotland, at the Highland Games, they throw a hammer, but it has a solid wooden handle and is thrown without turning. The hammer I had was an Olympic hammer, which has a long wire handle, and the thrower spins to get up speed before releasing it. He came and gave me one lesson, and he left behind his training books, which were in German, with photographs and diagrams of prewar German throwers.

To throw the hammer, it is necessary to have a six-foot cement circle. My father solved that problem by having the local blacksmith make a six-foot iron hoop, which they embedded in the ground and filled it with cement. Normally, the cement is quite rough, but the men who finished mine made it nice and smooth. Years later, when my old friend Peter came to throw, he said it was the fastest hammer circle in Britain. I threw so much the field looked like the Somme after a battle. A twelve-pound hammer thrown from about eighty meters away, coming down from a high arc, digs about a foot into the ground. I loved it. I was all speed and power and to hell with technique. The first time I threw in competition was at the Scottish Schoolboys. I lifted their record by seventeen feet.

Hammer throwing was not commonly done, but my father managed to find a club in Glasgow, where I would go when he could take me. It was only for competitions. It was far too far for training. In North American terms, it would be fairly close, but these were Scottish roads and ancient secondhand British cars, so it seemed like a long way.

The sports authorities in Scotland were good to me. Looking back, I still find it hard to believe how much whoever it was in Scotland who ran amateur sports looked after me. I got to go to weekend courses at a country house for elite athletes. It is difficult to think, after all these years, that I was an elite athlete who someone thought could go to the Olympics, all five feet, eight inches of me. I remember that one of the boys I once shared a room with got the bronze medal in the five thousand meters, I think, in the European Games. There never were any more than about thirty or so boys at these courses.

I was even invited to a Three *A*s course in England once. This was for the best kids in Britain. All the throwers I was training with at that meeting were about six feet, two inches. As in the throws, it is simply the principle of moments—the longer the lever, the more the power. I got by because I was faster and stronger.

There were female athletes there also, so one night, we had a dance. One of the instructors at the course was an English girl who had not only won the Olympic long jump but also was exquisitely beautiful. I danced with her. I was so tongue-tied I could not say anything. The next girl I danced with was a little blond girl who ran hurdles. After we had been dancing for a couple of minutes, she said, "You know nothing about women, do you?" I had to confess sadly that she was right. I guess that was the story of my life.

The British Schools Meeting was held in Scotland one summer. A big boy came up from England and won. His name was Peter Aston, and we had been friends ever since. He and a friend came home with my brother and me after that meeting. We lived in a big old manse, so finding a bed was not a problem. The next day, my mother cooked a Scottish breakfast, which I don't think Peter had ever heard of before. It was all eggs, sausages, back bacon, and black pudding—that is, a blood sausage. I have had it in Ireland and Germany, but nowhere else. It sounds awful but tastes great.

We spent the rest of the day throwing the hammer before he went back to London. He won the British Junior that year. He was a year older than I was, so next year, it was my turn. I was not expected to win because there was a boy who had thrown farther than I had. But I never ever had any nerves in a competition, so I won. I took the trophy back to Peter's house and left it with his mother. I was going to university anyway, so I did not really want it. When the organizers wanted the trophy, which was a huge silver affair, for the next year, I had told them that Peter's mother still had it in London.

What I do remember was that I went to Paris after that meeting. When I came back, the miniskirt, in all its glory, had arrived. The girls in London tended to be about a foot taller than the girls in Scotland, so on the underground, or subway, as it is called elsewhere, I couldn't but notice these Amazons with these tiny skirts and these incredible legs. Massimo, a man I once worked for in Italy, who had just been transferred from Rome to Milan, put my feelings in words. Surrounded by these models in Milan, he said, "A man could easily lose his mind."

I spent so long in the underground that I missed the train back to Scotland. Some things in life were more important than trains. The only other time I remember seeing such stunning women was when I was operating in a town in northern Italy called Bavenna. It was spectacular, being on one of these fabulous northern Italian lakes. I was doing a demonstration on knee replacement. I had never seen such audiovisual aids. They had throat mics, boom mics, several cameras, and a man sitting outside the operating room with a four-way split screen. Fortunately, the operation went well, and I did not use any bad words, which are fairly common in the operating room.

It was only when I had finished that they told me it was Piedmont Television, and it was going out on live feed. Apart from this knee meeting, Fiat, the Italian car company, was introducing a new, cheap car for sale in Eastern Europe. I assumed it was Poland because most of the dealers seemed to be Polish. I did not think much of the car, but Fiat had hired Italian models to sit on the cars. I had never seen such massed beauty in my life and never expect to ever again. One glimpse of paradise should be enough for a lifetime.

I still thought that I was going to the Olympics, so when it came time to go to university, I wanted a field that took a long time and was not too intellectually challenging. My brother, who was a physicist, suggested medical school because that was a six-year program in Scotland. I really wanted to be an engineer and build bridges, but the only people building bridges just then seemed to be the Japanese, and I thought it unlikely that they would hire a gaijin.

So I went to medical school and loved it. Coming to the end of my first year, I got into trouble. I was only five feet, eight inches, and the boys I was competing against were all over six feet. To compete, I had to be stronger than them. I could lift so much weight that from age thirteen until about a year after, I stopped lifting. I could not cross my legs; they were so bulky with muscles. I used to read about what powerlifters were squatting, and I remember thinking, *What sissies.* Then anabolic steroids became available. The tall beanpoles I was competing against put on twenty or thirty pounds of muscles in six months. I managed to get some, but it really didn't help me that much, as I was already close to what my body could take.

I developed pain in my knee. Initially, it was not bad, but it got worse, to where I could not sleep at night for about two years. My father took me round to half the orthopedic surgeons in Scotland, and no one could find anything wrong. In retrospect, I got lucky, as someone might have operated on me. I tried one leg squats for six months, which must have looked pretty stupid, but then I recognized the inevitable and gave up.

It was only when I was a resident in training in orthopedic surgery that I realized what my problem had been. I was sore for about seven years, and then the pain went away. I could not even remember which knee it was. I had had quadriceps tendonitis.

What that is, is a very tiny fracture of the tendon as it goes into the bone. You can find it with a microscope but not the naked eye. I actually did research on this when I was a resident. The head pathology technician at the cancer hospital was Scottish and vaguely related to my clan, and as we say in Scotland, "Blood is thicker than water." I had been told to find out the cause of tennis elbow by my professor Ted Dewar. I probably had been mouthing off with a new theory of mine, so he told me to prove it. This technician had golden hands. She could cut a whole section of a heel or an elbow to make a histology slide. I know this does not sound like anything, but it is. It simply cannot be done; no one has hands that steady, but she could. This was Michelangelo or Leonardo. I kept these slides for years but somehow lost them, to my infinite sorrow.

Once I could see the anatomy at microscopic level, the problem was obvious. As a tendon goes into a bone, it undergoes some changes. The change from tendon to bone occurs at a zone called the tidemark, because that is what it is. It is the area of the watershed where some blood is coming from the bone and some from the tendon, so the blood supply is very poor. Tendons and bones have minor breaks all the time, but they are tiny and heal rapidly. A minor break at the tidemark takes forever to heal because of the poor blood supply. I called it a low vascular inflammatory reaction when I published an article on tailbone pain, or coccydynia, which is pathologically the same as tennis elbow. So I knew what the problem was, but that did not help with treatment. I did develop an operation for tennis elbow, where I simply lengthened two tendons at the wrist, which worked just fine, but no better than the original operation at the elbow.

For quadriceps tendonitis, there is no treatment. Ice and stretch and all the rest of it help a little, but not much. The cases I see are tragic. They are mostly little girls who want to be professional dancers. They get quadriceps tendonitis, and they are out of dance for two years minimum until it heals. If you are out of dance for two years, you are out, period. The girls all know that, so this diagnosis always produces floods of tears.

Last year, they asked me to return to England to give the presidential address at the Hammer Circle Annual Reunion. I had not thrown a hammer since I went to Canada more than forty years ago, so I bought one. There was no place to throw, so I got up at 6:00 a.m. to throw in a park, which I am sure was strictly illegal. After almost dislocating a hip while turning with the hammer, I was somewhat afraid and did not exactly excel. I threw at the meeting, slightly less than the twelve-year-old girls. Who knew that women started throwing the hammer in the '90s? They were actually very graceful doing so, much more so than the heave and grunt of the other throws.

CHAPTER 4

SCHOOL

Did I like it or not? I cannot remember. Primary school was in the village, but for high school, I had to go to the local town called Falkirk. Other than the gym teacher, the only one I can really remember was Slim Somerville. He was the head of mathematics, and he was a wonderful teacher. He taught at the pace of the slowest in the class, but he ended every class five minutes early. He would call the three or four bright boys to the front of the class and give out math books, which had large sections of questions and answers. He would say, "Finish this book by next week. If you have problems, speak to me." I always thought that this was the way teaching should be, let the bright kids push themselves as hard as they like.

I doubt that it mattered very much anyway. My mother had advanced course books, and she sat with each child for one hour every night, going over their lessons. I had always been a voracious reader. My father said that I should read the French authors as soon as possible, because they were either so long-winded or unutterably sad, like Victor Hugo, that no one could read them as an adult. I read most of these books before age twelve. The only Victor Hugo book I even remotely liked was *L'homme Qui Rit*.

Poetry I liked. I have always had a good memory, a garbage-can mind. It is not an eidetic memory, where one look is enough. But if I really concentrate on it, I can remember it, more or less, forever. When I was sitting for my American board examinations in orthopedic surgery, one of my examiners was Dr. Crenshaw, the head of the Campbell Clinic. He had edited a textbook on orthopedic surgery, which all orthopedic residents used. This book has about a couple of thousand pages. I must have read it cover to cover at least five times during training. He asked me about a complication following hip dislocation. My answer was that "on page 422, first paragraph, of your book, it says this—"

He said, "That will be fine. Go and have a cup of coffee."

When I was writing this paragraph, I checked it. Forty years had passed since I last opened that book. I was wrong; today I thought page 622, but it was 422, so my memory is not infallible. I thought and still think that there is nothing like poetry. It is the story of mankind, written in a form that one can remember. I have always taken the position that if it is not memorable, it is of no significance. I talk in clichés and quotations because I believe that all there is to say has already been said by someone else, only better. Maybe you can train a mind or maybe you cannot; I do not know. But I certainly trained myself to learn poetry.

The sad thing is that poetry, as a genre, died in the mud of Flanders along with the flower of Europe. Poetry never recovered from that desolation. John McCrae, the man who wrote about the poppies, wrote the following:

> To you we fling the torch
> Be yours to hold it high'
> But there was no one left to hold it high. The great "might
> have beens," such as Grenfell, Hodgson, and the rest were
> gone.
> I have a rendezvous with death
> on some scarred slope of battered hill.

They certainly did, and the others who survived were so traumatized that all they had left was their bitterness. There were no more glad mornings. The world's last poet was T. S. Eliot, and even then, his greatest output was fairly minimal.

> Eyes, there are no eyes here
> In this valley of dying stars
> This hollow valley
> This broken jaw of our lost kingdom.

I still cannot fathom how utterly and completely poetry just disappeared. Maybe it is just hiding and will come back again, but I don't think so. It has been gone now for about one hundred years.

After the chore of reading all these unreadable French authors, I read the English, mainly Dickens, but I found others such as Hardy deadly dull. I did try the Russians, but simply could not. When we were children, my mother used to read Sir Walter Scott to us as a bedtime story. I thought they were pretty good and still think the basic plot lines are. As bloodthirsty little children, I especially remember Scott's book *The Fair Maid of Perth*, where Hector seduced the blacksmith's girl. There was the famous battle of the North Inch, where two Highland clans came down to fight it out in front of the king. There were forty men on each side. The clan Chattan, which is a cadet of the Camerons, was one man short, so the smith volunteered, because Hector was of the clan Kay. Gow Chrom, the bandy-legged smith, was the best swordsman and kept killing them, trying to get to Hector. Hector's godfather kept putting his sons in front, saying, "Another one for Hector."

Eventually, the Gow killed them all, and Hector ran away, which was a very satisfying denouement.

And then I found Kipling and the science-fiction authors and some of the historical-fiction people. I fell in love with these people and have never fallen out of love.

CHAPTER 5

MEDICAL SCHOOL

I went to a medical school in St. Andrews, the home of golf. I always thought of golf as an utter waste of time, a good walk ruined, as someone said; it sounds like Mark Twain. Admittance to medical school in Scotland in those days was quite different. I am sure it has changed, but then one got in for three reasons: one was pure academics; second was if the family was of medical doctors because, the reasoning was, the student knew exactly what he was getting into; and the third criterion was if the student was good at sports. The thinking behind was that there was not much difference between training for an athletic event or an examination.

I thought that the system worked pretty well. But in order to do so, there had to be a large failure rate. On the first day, the dean had all of us medical students line up.

"Look right," he said. "Now look left. One of you will not come back next year. It is your choice."

Being from a little provincial high school, when I heard my classmates speak, I thought I was in trouble. They were from all over, mainly from England, but also from Mauritius, Rhodesia, Bahamas, Trinidad, and other places. I thought they knew more than I did. So I turned on the tap.

I was never afraid of hard work. All I did at the university was train for my throwing and academics. At the end of the first year, the dean had us line up again. He said that we were not a very good year, with one or two exceptions.

"Well, Mr. Cameron," he said.

I knew then I was unstoppable. When my dreams of the Olympics faded with anabolic steroids and quadriceps tendonitis, I concentrated on my studies, not that I had much choice. I was a government scholarship boy. One failure and the scholarship went away. But I worked sixteen hours per day, fifty minutes every hour. There were very few class medals I did not get. Three of them I missed, in subjects I knew I was far ahead of the others, because my father went and died in the middle of my examinations, and I had to go and bury him. There was no such thing as compassionate leave in those days. I had thought I was pretty unemotional, so my failure to annihilate the opposition in these examinations came as a surprise to me.

We had some fun in school. The residence I stayed in for the first year or two was adjacent to a trout stream. Everyone was out there with their dry flies, trying to fish. There were so many fishermen that I think the fish were afraid of flies. But I had been taught by my father's gravedigger. I used big pike hooks, which are serious triple hooks, big enough to hook a man. I used to wait for the trout to swim over the hook and foul hook them through the belly. One of the boys in the residence was having an affair with the cook, so she used to cook them for us.

What we used to do was get drunk every Friday night, usually on cider, which was cheaper and more alcoholic than beer. We would then feel so bad the next day that we would work hard until the next Friday.

After three pretty good years in St. Andrews, our whole class went to Dundee to begin clinical work. Not quite the whole class, another 20 percent were thrown out after the third year. In spite of the fact that I had chosen medicine because I wanted to go to the Olympics, not save the world, I loved it, especially pathology. I always believed that that was the basis of medicine. Dr. Lendrum was the professor of pathology. In his first class, he produced a book and said that the examination would come out of this book and gave the pages. As far as I remember, it was only a few hundred pages, so that was chicken feed for me.

He said it was his class, and he would talk about what he wanted. The students could come or not. He did not care. He was absolutely fabulous. His main interest was ancient Greece, and that was what he talked about. Occasionally, he would talk about pathology, but largely he left that to his lecturers. I had taken ancient Greek in high school to get good marks because everyone knew it was easy, and it was. Within a few months, one could read Demosthenes in the original. The professor enjoyed a good argument, and I was quite happy to give him one, when I bothered to attend his classes. This was the first time I had met people who really adored intellectual challenges. I remember fighting with one of the pathologists. I kept insisting that I was right. The lecturer went off and got a book and pointed to the page and said triumphantly that I was wrong.

I once wrote a thesis for them, in which I argued that all cancers, except the obvious environmental ones like mesothelioma due to asbestos, were due to viruses. At that time, the only cancers we really knew about were due to viruses like the papilloma and a few others. It is interesting to note fifty years later that I was probably correct.

After degree examinations one day, I was walking down the street. A car stopped beside me, and a hand came out and shook mine. "We like people who impress external examiners," said Professor Lendrum.

I do not think there was any subject or any teacher I disliked in medical school. Whether that statement is real or just a rosy afterglow, I don't know. We had a system where, as medical students, we could fill in for interns and residents who were on holiday or somewhere else. I therefore worked most of the time. The practical training was done by nurses. Don't know how to sew someone up? A nurse will show you. Don't know what to do? A nurse will tell you. It was not doctors who taught us medical students how to deliver babies; it was midwives. A midwife in the UK is a nurse who has done another two years of additional training. I delivered thirty-two babies. I know because we had to live in the hospital for a month or two and keep our individual notebooks.

Marie Kidd showed me how to reduce fractures. She was from the Western Islands in Scotland and spoke the Gaelic language. So she spoke English in the singsong of the islands. She was about five feet tall and weighed about eighty pounds, and she was the sister in charge of the plaster room, where casts were changed and minor fractures were reduced. She would sit in the nursing station directing her subordinates. She smoked constantly and hardly ever saw the patients. She would look at the x-rays and tell me to reduce or straighten the fracture out. I was supposed to know how to do it, being a young doctor. So I would go off and reduce the fracture, get an x-ray, and show it to Marie. She would look at the x-ray and either OK it or say, "Na na, the chief would not be accepting that. Go do it again."

I never saw Marie Kidd flustered in her whole life. These women were wonderful. Meg Scrim was a tall, rail-thin lady. I am not sure she ever saw herself as a lady, but I did. There was not anything she could not tell us medical students to do. In the middle of the night, I would be reducing fractured femurs, drilling pins in, and establishing traction. She would not dream of calling the senior resident. She and the medical student could handle it, whatever it was. Or Alice Mundie, who was the sister in one of the wards I frequently worked. In those days, a sister answered to the consultant and to God, but to no one else. When I was covering her ward, we would meet for coffee in her office at 9:00 a.m. She had her own fancy china service and her silver coffeepot. She already had had her nurses' meeting and would then tell me.

"You have to see Mr. Smith, Mr. Jones, and Mr. Green. The rest are fine."

The orthopedic wards in Dundee were full of criminals. There were no jobs for men, so stealing was an occupation. Dundee was built on the side of a steep hill. The thieves would be ransacking a house. The police would come running in the front door, so the robber would jump out the back window. He would find himself two or three stories up and so would fracture his heel bone or calcaneus, which is the fracture one gets from a vertical fall.

The reason these nurses were so good was several fold. One was that there were not that many status jobs for women, and a sister was a high-status job, so these women were often as clever, if not more clever, than the doctors. Also, there was no advancement. Once a nurse became a sister, it was as far as she could go. The only step up was to be a hospital matron, the senior nurse in the whole hospital. This changed when I was a medical student. There was a report given to or commissioned by the central government that allowed senior nurses to enter hospital administration.

The advantage was that they were on a different pay scale, with endless promotions and increased pension benefits, so of course, they had to do it. No matter how much you love your job, economics has to be taken into account. This meant that all these fabulous nurses, in a short time, became second-rate administrators and effectively disappeared from nursing. I thought it was a tragedy then, and I think it was a tragedy now. If they wanted to pay them more, then pay them more, but don't change the job description.

Working in the emergency department was always fun. Dundee, at that time, was probably the worst slum in Europe. Perhaps Marseille ran it close, but nowhere else. The only jobs in Dundee were for women. The main job was weaving jute, which came from Bangladesh. The looms were so noisy that Dundee had its own accent, as the women all had high-tone deafness. They could not hear the vowel *i*, so it was *fev* in place of *five*, a *peh* rather than a *pie*, and a *teh* rather than a *tie*. When I was there, they brought in new looms. But these were noisier than the old ones.

Downtown Dundee was a good place to avoid, especially on a Friday night, unless you were really looking for trouble. Beatings and stabbings were common, but surprisingly, not too many people died. The nursing station in the emergency department was always full of police. Many of the nurses were married to policemen. They seem to have an affinity for one another. These were the old days when no one had heard of police brutality, so on second thoughts, I had best keep these stories to myself because some of them were bad. I will tell one though. One of my doctor-friends was a big man from Balochistan, so we called him Big Baloch. I was complaining to him one day that it looked as if the whole world was going to become Communist. He did not disagree, but he said, "If it all goes down the toilet, you can come out to Peshawar, and you and I can till the fields together."

I wanted to do ENT surgery, maybe because the two prettiest nurses were on the ENT floor, and one of them was a very junior sister, which of course meant she was very, very clever, always a big attraction. To my sorrow, however, when I tried to operate under a microscope, with significant magnification, I found that I had a congenital tremor. It was not visible to the naked eye, but under magnification, I could see the needle swing backward and forward like a metronome.

So then I thought I would like plastic surgery, the surgery of deceit, I heard it called. To watch a surgeon turn a monster into a human being was unbelievable. The central government had just brought in a bill so that the people in juvenile prison, some of whom would give children nightmares, could have corrective cosmetic surgery, so I saw some very interesting cases. The only problem was the smell of burned children. There is nothing worse in the whole world than that smell. I have a pretty strong stomach, but I could not take that, and looking after burned children is what a plastic surgeon does.

I therefore regretfully gave up the thought of plastic surgery, but I never really lost my love of it. I did a lot of revision (redo) surgery and was often faced with horrible scars, which I delighted in correcting. One famous lawyer I have consulted for many years got mad at me once because I cleaned up a terrible scar on one of her plaintiff's bottom. She was mad because she had planned on having the gentleman drop his pants in court and show the jury the extent of his injury. She was a great lawyer. I was once advising her on a case in which she was suing the government for icy roads in Northern Canada in the middle of winter. Believe it or not, she won.

She once fell downstairs and broke her ankle, so she came to my outpatient clinic the next morning. This was one tough lady, so she was not complaining much, so I thought that it would be a minor fracture only. When I got her x-rays, she had the type of fracture that needed to be stabilized surgically. I did not have any operating time that day, so I was busy calling in favors, trying to get OR time. I sat her in a wheelchair in one corner of my clinic.

The clinic I prefer is a big room with stretchers in each corner. There is nothing shameful about having a bad joint. It is not like having syphilis, which one might want to discuss in private. These patients all know one another as they come back for regular rechecks, just as one does with one's car. Experienced patients are very useful in helping patients who have never had surgery before.

I saw a patient who had a legal problem. A great lawyer was sitting there doing nothing, so I sent the patient to consult with her. The next patient heard this, and he asked if he, too, could speak to her. Word got around the clinic, and very shortly, the line up to see Fern was bigger than the line up to see me. I managed to get operating time later that day. Just before she went to sleep, she told me to leave a nice scar. She was justly very proud of her beautiful legs and would wear very short skirts at trial. Fortunately, the scar I left was nearly invisible.

Oh, she was, she is clever. Pain has always been one of my interests. She taught me so much about perceived pain. We actually published a research article in a major peer-reviewed journal on that topic, and I named a medical condition after her.

I finally decided on orthopedic surgery. The main reason was my lecturers. I filled in for interns and residents whenever possible, so I worked with a wide variety of people, and the orthopedic surgeons seemed the easiest men to get on with. Besides, orthopedics is just a form of applied engineering, which was what I wanted to do anyway.

CHAPTER 6

A DOCTOR, SORT OF

When medical students graduate, they have one further hurdle in their apprenticeship. They have to spend one year as an intern. I went to a large town in the north of England to do mine. The unit where I worked specialized in liver problems. When people have terminal cancer, it will often spread to the liver, so this unit had innumerable people dying of cancer. The problem was that the cancer would get into the spine, which would crumble away, leaving many patients in agony with every move they made.

Fortunately, they had this marvelous drug mixture I had never heard of before. It was called the Brompton cocktail. Brompton was a chest hospital in London. It was a mixture of morphine, which would relieve the pain; cocaine, which counteracted the sedative effect of the morphine and made the patients bright and alert; and chlorpromazine, which is a drug, or the original drug, to treat schizophrenia. This counteracted the nausea effect of the morphine and, I think, helped the anxiety and fear. I thought it was a wonderful way to slip into "that good night." Patients were bright and alert and could speak rationally and without fear to their relatives, then they quietly drift off to sleep.

Other than that unit, I had never been in the business of dying, but looking back more than half a century, I only hoped that something like the Brompton cocktail is available when it comes my time to pass on.

Being in a medical unit, I was exposed to things I usually never see. I remember one night a man came into the emergency department and left his mother. There was nothing medically wrong with her, except she was so old she could no longer function on her own. I was given orders to get rid of her. Eventually, I tracked down her son. I still remember this weary voice saying that he was a man on his own in his fifties, and he could not cope with his mother any longer. I did not know what to say then, and I don't know now.

I am sure we had Jews in Scotland, but I don't know that I ever recognized one. This town was the city in Europe possibly, and England certainly, with the highest proportion of Jews. I found that out when bodies kept disappearing. I would certify someone as dead. They were supposed to go to the coroner, but the body would disappear, to my amazement. The ward nurses eventually told me what was happening. Apparently, the ultra-Orthodox Jews are required to bury the body before sunset. The family would therefore simply come into the hospital, dress the corpse, and walk out with it.

My resident was a lady doctor. She was very, very clever. I did greatly admire her. I think I was in love with her. When she found out that I knew almost every decent love poem in the English language, she used to egg me on. I would tell her, "There be none of Beauty's daughters with a magic like to thee."

And she would say, "You can surely do better than that."

So I would try again, "Can a man stand upright in the face of the naked sun? Or a lover in the presence of his beloved? If my feet fail me, oh, Heart of my Heart, am I to blame being blinded by the glimpse of thy beauty?"

She thought it was hilarious. She was married to another doctor in the town and would never let me touch her.

Back in Dundee, I completed my internship. By this time, I knew I was going to Canada. The decision was made for me by one of my professors, George Murdoch. He was a very well-known amputation orthopedic surgeon, especially in the US, where he would consult for the DVA. He ran the Limb Fitting Center in Dundee. Quite a few famous people came to him for artificial limbs, including a well-known British fighter air ace, who had lost both legs in an accident before the Second World War and yet flew fighters in that war. As a medical student, I used to assist him in the operating room in some of the hospitals he worked. I always had a great time with George. He once organized a conference in Sweden to try to codify European splint and artificial limb terminology, so there were participants from all over Europe, especially Germany, including the famous Herr Krause himself. This man seemed to have trained every German shoemaker after the war, where he had sustained some awful wounds. Even in Canada, years later, the old European shoemakers would listen with awe when I told them I had met Herr Krause.

I do not think we ever got a unanimous opinion. It seemed to me that about all we got was Herr Krause saying *nein*. But that did not matter. This was the only major conference that had ever been held for shoemakers, splint makers, and artificial limb makers. It was really good fun, as most of these people toil in obscurity all their lives, and here was someone recognizing just how important they actually were. There was drinking and singing every night. One morning, George came in with a swollen hand. He had obviously broken his fifth metacarpal. This is called a boxer's fracture because that is the way it gets broken. George looked around and did not see any of the delegates with a bruise on his face, so he thought whoever he had hit did not matter.

I was with George when he was driving back from an operating session in a rural hospital. Someone must have turned down a research grant proposal, and he was in a foul mood.

"Boy, you have to leave this [expletive] country. Apply to Toronto, Miami, Seattle, and use my name."

I had never really thought about immigrating, but I nearly always do what I am told. I asked every other orthopedic surgeon at the university what to do. There were about eight of them. Every single one of them said to immigrate. They varied in where they suggested going. Some said Australia, some the US, and some Canada, but they all said go. I was quite stunned. When forced to think about it, Britain was in a terrible mess, with strikes and taxes and unemployment and general doom and gloom. I really could not see any reason to stay. So I did what George told me to do.

Kay Clawson in Seattle said to come and have an interview. Being a scholarship boy, the only way I could get to Seattle was if I swam the Atlantic. Gus Sarmiento, the chief in Miami, whom I got to know and like later, although we mainly fought at the podium at meetings, said to come and work for him; but as soon as I became a landed immigrant, they would draft me and send me to Vietnam. I was not too keen on that, so I went to Toronto. They said I would have to wait one year.

So I had one year off. The Scottish Home and Health Department gave me a scholarship to go to the bioengineering school in Strathclyde University in Glasgow. I went there to learn basic engineering because I felt that orthopedic surgery was simply applied engineering. What I needed to learn was "engineering speak" or the language engineers use when they talk to one another. I learned a great deal, which was very useful in later life. Some of the engineers I met there also immigrated, and I have known and worked with them in the USA intermittently ever since. I also learned—and this was very important—that engineering projects were a team effort. I never forgot that.

After six months, I felt I had learned all I wanted to at that time. I gave the money I had been given back to the Home and Health Department. I don't think anyone in the world's history has ever returned money to a government. They were so astonished that they sent someone to see me. I told them I was leaving to go to Canada and didn't feel it was reasonable to take their money.

They made the magnificent gesture of offering me research funding forever if I stayed in Scotland. That offer absolutely astonished me, and I left Scotland feeling pretty good about the land of my birth.

CHAPTER 7

THE ENDLESS SUMMER

For the first and only time in my life, for the six months before I left Scotland, I had no responsibility. I worked in emergency departments and operating rooms as I wanted. That spring and summer were endless.

Whiskey, cigarettes, and wild, wild women. I was young; we were young. It was 1971, and no one cared about anything. All my vacations at the university, I would work until I had enough money, then I would take off for Europe. That summer, I had lots of money.

I suppose there was crime in those days, but I never heard of it affecting a student. Because we had very little money, we would live in the slums of wherever we were. Once, I took a student flight to Vienna. I don't know where they got those planes. I think they were held together with bailing wire and chewing gum. The boy I was sitting beside on the plane was a student of fine arts from some university in England. We roomed together in a tiny room beside the central train station, the usual ultracheap place for students, and ate in a working man's café. His professor had given him a list of things he had to see. I went with him.

It was fascinating. He had to see one store that had a very avant-garde design. We had to go to this museum to look at chairs and that museum to look at something else and all sorts of other things that would never have crossed my mind to see. One afternoon, we walked out to the Schönbrunn Palace. We stopped for *ein grosse* lager at every bar on the way. We fell asleep on the front lawn and never did get inside the palace. In the USA, we would probably have been arrested, but being in Austria, no one cared.

I went to all sorts of weird places. In 1963, I spent a couple of months in Warsaw, working in City Hospital Number Five, which was very interesting. I remember one surgical case. It was an aortofemoral bypass, so the patient had his belly opened from top to bottom. At noon, everyone stopped working and went for lunch, leaving the patient wide open, with a nurse anesthetist only. This was new to me, but I was told that, at noon, all true Poles suffered from hypoglycemia, or low blood sugar, and needed to eat. So we ate and watched an American TV show, *Dr. Kildare*, on a tiny television with Polish subtitles and then went back and finished the case.

There were other interesting things, and I got to know Warsaw and Kraków. Flying was a different experience. One climbed up the stairs on the back of the plane, which was not level, and went up a sloping aisle to one's seat, which I thought was like the seat one sat on in school, bolted to the floor. The tray table was a slab of wood banged across one's knees by a stewardess, who clearly was a KGB jailer. Objections were not allowed.

As students, we mostly took the trains around Europe. What I would do was travel as far out as possible, buy a train ticket home, and then stay until I ran out of money. There was no need to eat on the way back. One could easily survive not eating for a couple of days, which was about how long it took from almost anywhere in Europe. There were memorable moments. Once, I took the train from Athens to Istanbul. This was a train full of students going home from a university in Athens. It needed two engines to get up over the mountains in the north of Greece, one pulling and one pushing. On the top of the mountain, we had to stop at a siding to let the fabled Orient Express go by. Someday I want to go on the Orient Express, but now I think it only goes from Paris to Vienna.

At the top of the mountain, they took the pushing train off, so we were in the last coach with the back door open, looking back down the track. We were drinking beer and throwing the cans out of the back. At every little stop, people would be selling skewers of roast lamb and beer. It does not sound like great fun, but it was. It does not take much to have a good time. Most spoke a little English, and I had my Attic Greek, which no one understood. There was a dark side to that journey. I don't know if anyone remembers the movie *Midnight Express*. That movie was true. I saw these poor, gullible, mostly US kids buying cardboard suitcases of hash from vendors who got on the train in Turkey.

Everyone tried to tell them not to do it. When the train stopped in Istanbul, on exiting the platform, there was a ring of police waiting for the cardboard-suitcase-carrying kids. Some of them were being pointed out to the police by the people who had sold it to them. Turkey was absolutely safe in those days, as the army was running things. One could stay in the cheapest hotels and eat anywhere. I walked the Galata Bridge, where one of my boyhood heroes, Mustafa Kemal, had disposed of his opposition. He hung them all from the lamp posts on the bridge, and the Galata Bridge is a long one. I also ate fish caught from the Golden Horn itself. I would take the ferry up the Dardanelles. The banks were covered by trees with incredible purple blossoms.

Drugs were beginning to be a problem in Europe. In Britain, drug addiction was seen as a personal tragedy, but it had nothing to do with the state. If one was an addict, one registered as an addict, and then one could get all the drugs one wanted free from certain pharmacies, mostly in London. It really was just heroin; there was nothing else. This of course meant that there was no money in drugs, so no criminals; and because of the unlimited supply, the addicts did not survive long.

The system seemed to me to work pretty well, accepting that it was, and still is, a personal tragedy. I believe that Portugal had adopted a similar scheme, and as a result, no one in that country was in jail for drug offenses. The British government, in its wisdom, on the basis of no science at all, decided that they could cure drug addiction. This was just a little optimistic as half a century later, no one has discovered how to cure drug addiction. I know of some interesting work with psychedelics, especially psilocybin, but that was in its infancy. The most successful scheme still seemed to be the drug version of Alcoholics Anonymous. What it did mean was that drug smuggling was in business before the ink had dried on that unfortunate piece of legislation. It also meant that all over Europe, the police began to search for drugs.

I was coming back from Morocco once and had the typical long hippy hair of the day. The Spanish policemen were searching the students. I was strip-searched. I could see the police officer put a rubber cot on his finger, and I was thinking, *Oh no, not that.* He did not do it, but that was enough for me. I had no interest in BOHICA. I had my hair cut short, and it remained short until it all fell out.

People were just so nice to students then. I was once in a train going from Lisbon to Seville. One Spanish boy and I had the compartment to ourselves. The boy obviously worked with his hands. We could not communicate very well. After a few hours, he pulled out his lunch, which was a loaf of bread and a large sausage. He used his pocketknife to cut them in half and gave the half to me. Another time, I was in Madrid. It was very busy as there was some sort of air show going on. I arrived very late at night, so I got a taxi at the train station. The driver tried a couple of hotels and then said they were all full, so he took me to his brother's house. For a dollar or two, they gave me a room for a night. In the morning, when I opened the shutters, I found I was on the top floor of a house, looking out over the red-tiled roofs of Madrid. I stayed with that family for about a week.

Treated with a modicum of courtesy, many taxi drivers are good people. When I first arrived in Toronto, I came by bus from Montreal, where I had got off the boat. I knew where I was working, so I asked a taxi driver at the bus station if he could find me a clean, cheap hotel close to the hospital. He did, and it was everything I asked for. I told him I was just off the boat, and he said he was not that long off the boat himself from Italy. I tried to tip him, giving him some coins, but he said that that was too much and that ten cents was more than enough. I knew then I had come to the right country.

I had so many great times in Europe. One of my father's friends was a Belgian who lived in Oudenaarde. When I was coming back from Europe, I tried to spend a day or so with him. The old man and I used to walk around the town square in the evening, having some of that superb Belgian beer. The last place we would stop was a café owned by a First World War veteran, Tommy, who had never gone back to Britain after the war.

I thought the song of that era, at least for me, was "Wand'rin Star," sung by Lee Marvin.

> Wheels are made for rolling, mules are made to pack
> I never knew a place that didn't look better looking back
> Homes a place for coming from, dreams of going to
> Which with any luck will never come true
> I was born under a wandering star.
> and.
> Do I know where hell is, hell is in hello
> Heaven is farewell forever, it's time for me to go.

CHAPTER 8

ROBIN DOWN THE LOGGING ROAD

Rudyard Kipling said this:
Robin down the logging road
Whistles come to me.
Spring has found the maple grove
The sap is running free.
All the winds of Canada
call the ploughing rain.
Take the flower and turn the hour
And kiss your love again.

I left Britain from Liverpool aboard the *Empress of Canada*. The thinking was that "everyone hates new things for a while." There was a lot I was leaving behind in Scotland, not least was the promise of endless research money. If I were to fly out, then if I disliked it, which I thought was inevitable, it would be easy to fly back. I knew enough people who had done that. If you take the migrants' boat, you know it is forever. There were all sorts of tales told of immigrants. The Australian one was that you could tell the difference between a planeload of Brits from a planeload of anyone else because when you turn the engine off, the plane continues to whine. The Canadian one was the thousand-dollar cure. You hate Canada after you get there, so you go home. You then realize why you left in the first place and go back to Canada. This costs one thousand dollars, or did in those days. You never want to go home again, so you are cured.

This was one of the last regular immigrants' boats from Europe. Pierre Trudeau, who became the prime minister of Canada, put a stop to it because for political reasons, he did not want European immigrants. When the boat left, the band played the immigrant's song, "'Tis not the leaving of Liverpool that makes me long for thee."

I shared a cabin on the bottom deck of the boat with three other men. The boat was full of young people my age, going off to the New World with the dreams of fame and fortune. Everyone was going there to work like a dog and be a success at something. That feeling was palpable. For some reason, I had thought that there would be long talks on the decks under the tropical stars. I should have looked at a map. It was fairly rough weather, so there was little time on deck. And before the boat came close to Newfoundland, we were meeting icebergs, so there were concerns about the *Titanic*. We came up the St. Lawrence River to Montreal, and then I took a bus to Toronto. I still remember that bus ride down the Highway 401. It seemed endless to someone coming from tiny Scotland with its tiny, narrow roads.

The Canada I came to was better than my wildest dreams. Everything was great. The roads were great, the women were great, and even the food was great. The first meal I ate in Canada was in a diner. The lady who owned the St. Leonards Hotel on Wellesley Street, where I went to for the first night, suggested the diner at the end of the street. It had tiny jukeboxes on each table, and they had this fabulous side dish called coleslaw. I had never had that before and love it to this day.

There were some things I simply could not believe. A man I was with got out of his car and didn't lock it. I pointed out to him that he had forgotten to lock his car. He said that this is Canada, and we don't need to lock cars or houses here. The only other place I found that was in Singapore. I was having dinner with a surgeon I had known for years. He forgot to lock his Porsche, which I pointed out to him.

"We don't bother to do that in Singapore."

"Don't they steal cars here?"

"Yes, but only once."

Singapore at that time was run by Mr. Lee, who was a serious man. There, it was a five-hundred-dollar fine for spitting on the street. Chewing gum was illegal. Taxation was a flat 10 percent. In spite of being one of the biggest seaports in the world, crime was quite low. Mr. Lee used to say about murderers that they were no use alive, so they might as well make some use of them dead. My friend was late that night because he had been up in Changi jail doing a bone harvest—that is, taking a bone for grafting, from what he called a double header. Mr. Lee had just had a couple of murderers executed. By the time they had finished harvesting hearts, livers, kidneys, corneas, and all, there wasn't much left.

The amazing thing about Canada was everyone helped. I do not include bureaucracy. That is the same worldwide. Bombelli in Italy said it best, "If you come up to a government man's workstation, he will say no before you even get there."

Renato Bombelli had a slightly pessimistic view of the world. He kept a packed suitcase just inside the front door of his villa for more than thirty years because if Italy ever voted in the Communists, he and his family would be across the border at Chiasso into Switzerland in less than half an hour. For the younger people who don't believe it, this was a real concern in Italy for years after the war, especially when everyone came to know the true horror of Communism, which incredibly did not seem to bother the European communist parties and, even more amazingly, present-day Marxists.

Another European friend said the same thing. Philippe Cartier, who was a great French unicompartmental knee replacement surgeon, told me that in Paris, no one works.

"The government man never works, and the right-wing man can't get to work because of the traffic."

Philippe was a great friend of mine. We were once at a teaching meeting on the island of Jersey. At the awards ceremony, they announced an award for the best talk given in "almost English." Philippe, who had taught himself English by listening to tapes in his car in the Paris traffic jams, spoke pretty good English, but I could see him scrunching up his face at the thought of this insulting award. The men from Memphis who had arranged the meeting were not fools. They gave the award to me.

Phillipe and I used to run a course on knee replacement in Athens once a year for about seven years, when knee replacement was just beginning and very few people knew how to do it. It was at the KAT Hospital. I taught total knee replacement, and Philippe taught uni knees. We used to have a great time in the Plaka, a collection of tiny streets and bars, where we used to drink and dance the Greek dances. The last time I was back in Athens, the Plaka was gone. It was simply a big hole in the ground. I suppose it is progress, but I am not sure.

At the last teaching session we had, the Greek surgeons told Philippe and me that we did not need to come back to Athens because they now knew how to do the operation. I can't think of a higher compliment than that. Philippe and I were having a drink beside the hotel pool when he told me that we were Texans. I told him that he had drunk too much and that he was from Paris and I was from Scotland. *"Non, non, mon ami,"* he said, "you do not understand. Texas is not a place. It is a state of mind."

I told this story much later to a lady from San Antonio, who absolutely agreed with Philippe. She was so pleased she sent me enough Lone Star T-shirts to last for a decade. Philippe always had an admiration of America, which was not usual in a Frenchman. He had learned to speak English because he felt he would never amount to anything if he could not talk to Americans. He pointed out that they had no interest in ever speaking anything other than English.

Another friend of mine felt the same thing. I was speaking at the Korean National Orthopedic Meeting in Seoul many years ago. It was chaired by an old friend of mine, Yoon Soo Park. He announced that from now on, all talks had to be given in English, because he said, "No one is ever going to learn Korean." A funny example of the same thing was at another meeting where I was a guest lecturer. This was the Hong Kong Orthopedic Meeting, which was held immediately after the transition, when Hong Kong left British rule and was returned to China. All the Hong Kong surgeons had been trying to learn Mandarin, which is the official language of China. In Hong Kong, they mostly spoke Cantonese. The surgeons would start of their talks in Mandarin, but after a few minutes, they would give up and revert to English.

I have always had a very Scottish accent. In Scotland, I felt I spoke with not much accent, not like the Glasgow or Aberdeen people. I learned differently when Dragon, a speech recognition program, first came out. I found it impossible to slave it to my accent. There is a hilarious video clip out there of two Scotsmen in a voice-activated elevator. The elevator doesn't understand which floor they are asking for. It is not that funny. It is real. Even now the voice-recognition technology still has problems with my accent. If I speak with a grossly exaggerated Indian accent, it can understand, but with mine, it has problems.

A large number of Scottish junior doctors always sat for some of the American examinations, just in case. The first one was called the ECFMG, the English something for foreign medical graduates. This was a test of the English language. A lady would read out a sentence, and we had to do something with it, to show we could understand English. The only problem with the exam I sat was that the lady came from South Texas, and I had great difficulty understanding what she was saying. I suspect the Americans did it on purpose. Americans never knew or cared much about Canada. On one of the first talks I ever gave in the US, I was introduced as "Dr. Cameron from Canada, as you can tell from his accent."

CHAPTER 9

TORONTO THE GOOD

When I arrived in Toronto, I found some strange things that took some difficulty understanding. They had, and still have, things called liquor stores. If one wanted alcohol, one went to one of these government stores where a piece of paper was filled out. The desk clerk then disappeared behind closed doors and came back with one's purchase in a brown paper bag. It was all very mysterious, and it took me some time to understand it. I still don't understand the rationale. The government insists it can sell liquor better than anyone else. This is strange because it cannot do anything else better than anyone else.

Not long after I had been in Canada, I was entertaining a young lady from Hungary. We were both immigrants. I was looking for something to drink with her. I passed by this shop that had a sign saying that they had Tokay for sale for $1.50. Tokay is the famous dessert wine from Hungary, and it is never for sale in Europe for $1.50. So I marveled and bought it. I made sure the bottle did say Tokay. When I opened it in front of her, I found it was some sort of foul, sweet sherry-type liquid. One wouldn't call that wine. I was extremely embarrassed.

When I explored this peculiar phenomenon, I found that they made wine in Canada from the *labrusca* grape, which is a sort of not very good eating grape. The wine produced was said to be "foxy." As I have never eaten or had relations with a fox, I would not know, but that stuff was awful. One would not even cook with it. For some reason, the government let the local producers of this dreadful stuff sell it in shops other than their own liquor stores. Probably because no one would buy it.

Eventually, one man did develop a hybrid grape, which would grow in Ontario, the Marechal Foch varietal, which did make a drinkable wine, and now there are several. The only problem was that in order to support local growers, the government put a floor price on wine. This meant that perfectly good, or sort of reasonable, wines from Europe that used to sell at two dollars or less suddenly cost seven dollars, which they were definitely not worth. As the Canadian wines were not worth seven dollars either, no one bought it, so the government, in all its magnificent wisdom, simply made the winemakers in France and the Napa valley wealthy. Oh well, at least the government tried. Intelligence was not treasured by the political class, and still is not. I had been in Canada for a few months when I took the train from Toronto to Montreal. It took four hours, which I thought was not too bad. Forty years later, I took the same train, and it took four and half hours, which is what one would expect from a government-run organization.

In Toronto, somehow the local government forgot to build any new subway stations for about fifty years, and they still do not know how to coordinate traffic lights. If there was an accident on one of the local highways, the police would close the road and would remain closed all day until they finish investigating it. Perhaps someone forgot to tell them that it has been no-fault insurance for the last thirty years. In Chicago, hardly the best-run city in the world as all its mayors seem to end up in jail, it takes fifteen minutes to clear the highway from downtown out to O'Hare. Perhaps that is the secret. Maybe we should put our mayors in jail. It would certainly be a better place than where most of them end up. It is said that Montreal runs on corruption and Toronto runs on incompetence. There has been one good mayor since I have been in Canada, or at least he was good when he was sober, and he was sober during the day when work got done. It was only during these interminable meetings, which would go on all night, on such vital issues as a street name that he got drunk, and who could blame him?

The level of competence can be gauged by a couple of occurrences. They were building new streetcar tracks. They were also buying new streetcars. The new streetcars were about thirty feet longer than the old ones. These geniuses of city planners built the boarding platforms for the size of the old cars, and it took them years to build a few miles, bankrupting the shop owners along the whole of that route. When they had finished, the new streetcars began to arrive, and lo and behold, who would credit it that the platforms were thirty feet too short. Who could have predicted that? The platforms all had to be rebuilt. What was even better was, they raised the streetcar tracks, except where they cross roads. I guess that they forgot that it snows in Canada, because when it snows, the streetcars cannot get up the slight rise onto the elevated track, so the streetcars stall in the middle of the road. Another fit of genius was that one contractor installed a bridge upside down. One would have thought that that might produce something called a penalty. One would have thought wrong. The contractor got a bonus and further contracts. I suppose they mean well, which is all that counts. The Toronto City Council operates like "every child gets a trophy" day. But one must forgive the vagaries of the political class, it keeps them off the welfare rolls.

CHAPTER 10

PATHOLOGY RESEARCH

What I always loved was research into anything. I once wrote a scientific paper with one of my female students, on the production of head deformities in various tribes, such as various flat heads or even a figure of 8 head produced in Europe. I think I called that paper, "Alas, Poor Yorick." I often wondered if someone had not done a little something to the head of Nefertiti. The impetus for that was when I was in North Bay, I bought from a trapper a skull of a wolf that had had a piece of wood jammed across its upper jaw when it was an infant. It had produced a wondrous deformity. I also wrote a research paper on the jaw joint of the longnose gar because it seemed to have ball bearings in that joint, which occurs nowhere else.

For one glorious six-month period when I was doing orthopedic pathology, I think my boss and I published about one research paper a month. I got to do orthopedic pathology because I knew the man I wanted to work for, and I begged Uncle Ted Dewar, who was the big professor who ruled all our lives. I knew I was, what we call in North America, a "pain in the ass," but Uncle Ted would not let them beat on me too hard. He gave me the best job, or the most prestigious job in Canada, at the Toronto General, when that was still the biggest and best hospital in Canada. It was called the Big House. He said to me, "Cameron, you have the personality of a shit, but I am giving you a job anyway."

I studied orthopedic pathology with Victor Fornasier, who was an Italian Canadian. I already had a background in pathology because I

41

loved that subject when I was with Professor Lendrum in Dundee. I had had another stroke of luck. There was a famed pathologist, John Barry, in Toronto. I had been in Toronto for about a year when I met him, because he used to give Wednesday lunchtime teaching rounds at Jim Bateman's hospital about once a month. I went to these rounds because I liked Jim Bateman. He was persona non grata in Toronto because he had been a doctor with the Canadian Armed Forces when they first went overseas in the Second World War. Because he was one of the first to go out, he was one of the first to come back. Naturally, he was resented for that. He had been trained as a neurosurgeon, and when he was faced with all these terribly wounded veterans, he began to do nerve repairs on the brachial plexus. He could do things that no one else could, and so no one believed him, except for his patients. When he opened his own hospital with Dr. Wright, another veteran, it was staffed with these maimed patients, to whom he had restored to some function.

As a resident, I once had to listen to a lecture given to us by a neurosurgeon I despised. He spent all his time disparaging Jim Bateman for his brachial plexus surgery, simply because he could not do it. When the great French surgeon Millesi began to publish on surgery similar to that which Bateman had been doing since the late '40s, this jackass began to set himself up as the big Toronto expert.

I was not of Toronto, so I had none of the homegrown prejudice, and I liked Big Jim. Stephan, his hospital chef, used to make the best sandwiches I ever ate for these Wednesday lunchtime teaching sessions, which were run by radiologist John Munn, who was also a great orthopedic teacher. I used to sneak out of the hospital I was working without telling anyone and go to these rounds, which I thought were the best in the city.

For a year or two, I spent every Thursday evening with the pathologist John Barry. He would buy me supper, and then we would look at histology slides of hips for a couple of hours or more. He had described all sorts of firsts, including labral tears, geode formation, etc. This will not mean much to the non-orthopedic reader, but this was and still is of significance.

Given this background, the six months I spent with Victor were unbelievable. I met Isobel Urquhart, the histology technician with the golden hands who could cut slides of anything. Some of my first work when I came to Canada was to classify arthritis of the hip. I was given thousands of x-rays of arthritic hips. I worked till after midnight most nights (did I ever mention that I was never afraid of hard work?) and was able to come up with a useful classification. During that time, one of the pathologists at an old people's hospital allowed me to dissect the hip joint of the cases on which he was doing an autopsy. Dissecting a fresh cadaver is very different than what is usually available, so I learned a lot more about the anatomy of the hip.

My main work with Victor Fornasier was on the early development of arthritis of the hip. I violently disagreed with a Boston surgeon who was working in the same field, and the upshot was that I was invited to address Grand rounds at Harvard in the Massachusetts General, probably one of the most famous hospitals in the world.

Europeans will not believe this. I was an assistant resident at that time. In the pecking order, an assistant resident is slightly above the man who cleans the toilets, but not by much. Only in America would an assistant resident be asked to be a sort of visiting professor to any university, let alone Harvard. I always loved that about the US. It did not matter who you were or where you were from; it was only what you did that mattered.

I was once at a research panel in the US, and everyone there was a big professor. The reason I was there was because it was pretty much my work that was under discussion. I was still only a resident. I was "mouthing off," because I knew what I was talking about, and no one else did. Residents do not "mouth off" to full academic professors, so people were getting annoyed. Then Chuck Townley stood up. Chuck was famous for his bad temper and his absolute inability to suffer fools gladly. He was also famous as one of the very original pioneers of knee replacement surgery.

I knew Chuck because he had had a scientific exhibit showing some of his research at the American Academy Meeting, and I had one in the next booth. No one seemed terribly interested in what Chuck had discovered or theorized, except me. I thought he was absolutely correct and spent a long time talking to him. Underneath that gruff exterior was a gruff interior but a clever interior. Cleverness has privileges. I thought Chuck's theories on knee replacement; indeed I thought almost everything Chuck ever said was probably correct. Chuck stood up at that meeting and said, "You should listen. The boy is probably right."

Victor and I were invited to speak at the Italian Orthopedic Meeting. He and his wife were already in Europe. My girlfriend and I flew into Amsterdam, and Victor picked us up. We wandered through Europe. We actually did not wander that much as Victor was a very fast and very good driver.

Incidentally, I only was with two really good drivers. One was a Canadian salesman. He would race cars in his spare time. He once picked me up at the airport in Zurich. We were going to a mountaintop meeting in the Swiss Alps. He had a good car. He asked me if I had ever done 150 miles per hour before. I told him I had not. He said we were doing that, and we had just passed a police car! Fortunately, we were so far ahead by the time the policeman got up to speed; he had time to pull off the road and hide up in the mountains. The other was when I had to go from Milan to the Rizzoli Institute in Bologna. I was driven by an outfit called the Blue Limousine. It was supposed to take about three hours, and this driver managed it with half an hour to spare. He almost never touched the brakes. I have never had such a smooth ride.

When I think about it, there were other times. I was once being driven into Paris by my friend Peter Aston. Peter was driving. He got something in his eye, so he took out his contact lens. He said that on French roads, you must never show fear. He did not take his foot off the accelerator. His wife, Carole, leaned over from the back seat and steered while still talking to my girlfriend until he put his contact lens back in.

Hans Willert, the great German surgeon scientist, once picked me up at the airport in Frankfurt, where he was still working before he became the professor in Göttingen. He said we should have a good dinner, so he drove halfway up the Rhine Valley.

I was saying to him, "Hans, are we not going a little quickly?"

"No, no. We are only doing two hundred kilometer per hour."

I actually was with Hans several times. I was with him once when we went looking for a new spargle, the year's first asparagus, which was a great delicacy in Germany. We found it close to the East German border. He and I ate asparagus, looking at the manned watchtowers of that monstrous tyranny.

Speaking of that, I was in Braunschweig the night the Wall came down. I was at one of these German dinner meetings where people sat and ate at long tables. At midnight, the news came that the Wall was down. Two million East Germans came across the border that night. The bartenders were selling the drinks a par for the ostmark, which was worth about ten cents to the deutsche mark.

On the way to the Italian meeting with Victor, we stopped at the Oktoberfest, which was going on in Munich. Victor had a friend there, so we had a few beers. There were so many visitors that there were no hotels available, so we drove on. We finished up high in the Austrian Alps in a little guesthouse at the head of a pass. In the morning, I could hear the cowbells ringing, and the view of the sweep down the valley was evocative.

That day, we made it to Ravenna and then over to the Apennines. On the way, we drove into a small ruined castle. As we drove in, the car pitched up over the threshold, and in the beams of the headlights, we saw a fresco high on the interior wall of the gatehouse. If we had not taken a car in there, we would never have seen it. The castle had been completely stripped, probably centuries ago, but obviously no one knew the fresco was there. We tried to think of a way we could possibly take it with us, because no one would know, but we could not come up with any way of doing it. I bet that it is still there.

We spent a day in Udine, which was the home of Victor and his wife. The only thing I remember about it was that people there were still speaking about how the Russians came through during the final phases of the war and hung a man on a meat hook. As this was about twenty-five years after, it must have left quite an impression on the people.

To get to the island of Sardinia, we took the ferry from Civitavecchia to Olbia. It was hunting season, and a fierce hunting dog was tied to every rail on the ferry. In the morning, when we drove down to Cagliari, it was like the Western Front; there were so many guns going off. I would not have liked to be a game bird in Sardinia that morning.

CHAPTER 11

ENGINEERING

I have always liked working with engineers. What you see is what you get. Shortly after my arrival in Toronto, I began to work with Bob Pilliar. He was developing the concept of fixing metal to a bone by making it porous so that a bone could grow in, thus holding it in place. He had started to work with Ian Macnab, who was a famous spine surgeon. I was Dr. Macnab's research fellow then. I spent the next several years defining the parameters of what is now the commonest method of fixing implants to the bone. Other work on this field was being done by Brånemark in Scandinavia, and Jorge Galante in Chicago.

This was absolutely new, so all sorts of experiments were necessary. We had money for research, but it was never enough. Animal work was crucial. Where possible, I used rabbits, but they were awfully small, and I was never sure how well rat and rabbit work translated into humans. This was in the early '70s, and at that time, a B-grade pedigree beagle, which was what I mostly used, cost $120. One could either use a lot of pound dogs or a few pedigree to get the same statistical data. As our usual research grant was about $10,000, this did not leave much. Each experiment therefore had to be carefully thought out to produce a yes or no answer, in order to limit the numbers involved.

The lady who was the head of the animal lab in the Hospital for Sick Children, where I did most of the work, was invaluable. I could not have done it without her help. I was mostly a resident in Toronto General, just across the street, so I used to run across whenever I could and get some work done. I was a full-time resident then, so time was very short. Even after I went on staff, I carried on with the same research. She was just so helpful. She would acquire dogs for me when others had finished with them.

The other person was a histology technician, who is now dead, so I can tell you what we did.

A histological slide of bone is expensive to make. Then it cost about twelve dollars per slide. I needed them by the hundreds. This technician used to put my slides through with patient numbers on them so that the government would pay for it, not me. If we had been found out, we would certainly have been fired, and considering the actual dollar amount, we may be jailed. These women were just so brave. They put it all on the line because they thought the research I was doing was important.

Once, I did a pig. It was about twenty pounds when I did it, but when the time had come to sacrifice it, it weighed about eighty pounds. The pig got loose. Pigs are smart. It knew something bad was going to happen, so there was no way it was going to go quietly. We eventually got it penned in the corner of the lab. We were looking at it, and it was looking at us—stalemate. Fortunately, Spyro, the man who cleaned the floors, was an old Greek wrestler. Spyro approached the pig with a wrestler's stance and threw himself on it. There was then a terrible noise, as pigs squeal very loudly, which was a concern as this was the top floor of the children's hospital. Spyro eventually pinned the pig. I never did another one.

People complained about animal work, but it had to be done. About thirty or forty years ago, the Swedes developed a technique of growing cartilage cells. It was thought that this stem cell research could be used to cure arthritis and everything else that ails the human body. The cells would grow just fine, but as soon as they reach the surface, they would be rubbed off. We were playing around with a matrix we could fix to the bone through which the cartilage cells would grow. One engineer who hung out with us developed a very good matrix of polyester, which did perform very well in the tissue culture lab, so I tried it on animals. Unfortunately, mammals have tissue esterases, which break down polyester, so that did not work. I never published that because it was and is difficult to publish negative results.

I should have. A few years later, I was in Europe visiting hip surgeons. I found one surgeon who had developed a hip with a polyester bearing. He had inserted one thousand before they began to fail. When I visited him, his *oberarzt* had revised 750 with 250 to go. I learned my lesson—always publish negative results no matter how stupid it makes you look.

There was a whole group of engineers based at a sort of think tank called the Ontario Research Foundation. I used to hang out with them. They all had other jobs, but they would find the time to do some blue-sky thinking and some work with me, if we thought of anything interesting. Bob Pilliar was a metallurgist. His main job was to develop Chobham-type armor for tanks. So he had this really big gun from the military. Bob White, one of the engineers, developed a pretty good artificial shoulder when none of the ones on the market worked well. It never sold very well, which taught me a lesson that the world does not beat a path to your door and that nothing sells itself. Bob White and I developed a multidirectional screwdriver, which I sent off to Switzerland, where the trauma systems were being developed. I never heard back from Switzerland, but a couple of months later, an identical design became available for sale. It probably was coincidence, but I have a little suspicion.

Waterloo was a great engineering school in Ontario. The professor of civil engineering Greg McNeice came to see my boss Ian Macnab. He had developed a form of mathematical analysis, which he felt he could apply to artificial joints. I was told off to liaise with him. It was fascinating, and some of the things I knew began to make sense. Just because you know something to be the case does not mean you understand why. We spent a lot of time working on it. Greg eventually took a year's sabbatical, which he spent with Harlan Amstutz at UCLA. There he made contact with a US engineer, Tom Gruen. They worked out the modes of failure of cemented hips, which was a major step forward. When he came back to Canada, I kept in close contact with Waterloo and eventually became an adjunct professor for a while so that I could supervise the theses of some of the students. I would also lecture once a year or so to the mechanical engineering class.

A new form of microscope had been developed—a scanning electron microscope. It was magic. For the first time, one could see things at high magnification in 3-D. This opened up a completely new world. The professor of civil engineering at the University of Toronto gave me access to his department's scope. I got access from 9:00 p.m. until 11:00 p.m. or midnight a couple of times a week. He gave me a technician to run it for me, and he did not charge me anything.

I would finish doing the bulk of the emergency surgery by about 8:00 p.m., then I hustle over to the U of T's Wallberg Building, where the scanning scope was housed. They were within five-minute walk of each other, so I could still be on call. I know this generosity sounds a bit far-fetched, but it was true. It is no longer, as research has fallen prey to those who administer research but do not do any themselves. To further add to the sense of unreality, my intern for six months, Wally Peters, who later became famous for sorting out the fake claims about silicone breast implants, had his own laboratory, where he was doing research on burns. As very junior members of the university, the bottom of the food chain, in the evening I would go to my giant scope, and he would go to his own burn lab.

John Medley was the professor of mechanical engineering at Waterloo. I met with him initially because he had a bad hip. When he was younger and footloose and fancy-free, he rode a motorcycle around South America. In one town, he was run down by a car and sustained a severe fracture of his hip. The passersby ran to him; he thought they were to give him aid. He was wrong. They ran to him and stole his wallet and other possessions. He did a year sabbatical in Leeds, which had then, and still has, an excellent bioengineering school. I do not know how much he learned there, but he did something worthwhile. Sir John Charnley, the principal developer of the artificial hip, had a very good engineer called Jude. John Medley stole Jude and brought her back to Canada and married her.

When I replaced his hip, he got a couple of his own engineering students to come to the operating room to record on video the operation. He would show that when he was lecturing on applied engineering. He was one of the experts on orthopedic bearing materials, and we used many of his test machine over the years, especially for fatigue testing, which is extremely time-consuming, as anything under a couple of million cycles is almost meaningless. For more than twenty years, he used to bring a couple of his students a couple of times a year to watch me do joint replacement surgery. The students really liked that. Unfortunately, about ten years ago, some second-rate administrator with nothing else to do decided that there were privacy issues. It did not matter that the patients gave consent. Administration, in all its magnificent wisdom, decided that there was something secret about the inside of a patient's knee. What that secret is quite escaped me and the patients, who used to talk quite happily to the engineering students before they went to sleep.

Oh well, who can complain about the march of social progress? Or, complain all you want, but the octopus of bureaucracy grows bigger every year.

CHAPTER 12

SURGICAL TRAINING

The orthopedic program in Toronto was quite famous. It had been started by a Dr. Gallie and was one of the first comprehensive programs in North America. It lasted five years, with the first year being a year of research. The residents were more or less on call every second day for five years. No one complained. If anyone had, they would have been tossed out. Surgeons were not expected to fray around the edges. We were all hungry for surgery. I remember almost coming to fisticuffs with another senior resident at 2:00 a.m. over a case. He claimed I was off duty, so it was his, but I pointed out the patient had come in before 5:00 p.m. when I was still on call.

Most specialized surgery consists of a few different types of cases. After all, there's only so much you can do inside a belly. Orthopedics, however, has a vast assortment of operations, and as residents, we wanted to try them all. Currently, we laugh at how little surgery the new doctors do compared with us, as they are now on call a couple of times a week only. The old European surgeons like the great Robert Judet used to laugh at how little surgery I had done compared with himself.

I did not like most of the non-orthopedic surgical training, especially neurosurgery. These surgeons were so slow it drove me crazy with boredom. There is nothing very interesting in spending hours inside a patient's head. I did six months of neurosurgery next door to the cancer hospital, so we frequently had emergencies. The patients would have secondary tumors in the spine. They would bleed into the tumor, which would swell, or the bone would collapse and the patient would be paralyzed to add to their dreadful woes. The pressure had to be taken off the spinal cord within a fairly narrow time frame, so these cases had to be done as an emergency. I already had done a fair amount of spine surgery with Ian Macnab, so I was pretty quick at it. The neurosurgeons were so slow that I would only call them when the patient was asleep and prepared for surgery, so by the time they got to the hospital, I had pretty much finished the case.

Eventually, I was the senior resident in Toronto General. This was when it was still a level 1 hospital. That meant it could take all emergencies. The professor saw it as his duty to take all the cases no one else could do or wanted to do, which was wonderful for teaching residents. Professor Dewar had not operated himself for several years. His senior resident did the surgery. That doesn't sound good, but by the time a resident has reached that status, he should be an automaton. When the professor says to make a cut of ten centimeters long and two centimeters deep, the resident does it. Talking him through an operation should be simple. After all, in another year or so, he will be on his own.

What I liked were nights. The consultants had gone home. We only called them in if it was something we could not handle, which was about zero. There were a lot of subway jumpers. When the subway is delayed, think of a jumper. This was never publicized as it would inevitably lead to me-too suiciders. If a jumper survived, they usually lost a limb or two. It was our job to put the limb back on. The other cause of limb loss was motorcycle accidents. We called them motorcycle donor cycles because that was where the organs for donation came from, as the accident victims were usually young, fit, healthy males.

There were many nights spent doing this. I know it sounds awful, but I liked it. As the senior orthopedic resident, I had to rapidly join the two bones together to fix the arm or leg back on. The senior vascular resident, who was Tyrone David, who subsequently went on to become a world-famous cardiac surgeon, would repair the arteries and veins. Nancy McKee, who was the senior plastic surgical resident, would then tag the nerve ends for later repair or, in rare instances, do an immediate nerve suture. When they had finished, I would have to tidy everything up and close it. That does not sound like fun, but it was. I felt I was privileged to spend a few hours with a couple of great surgeons.

I was able to sit my examinations a year earlier than the other residents in my year because I got an early rotation in the children's hospital, so I had fulfilled the requirements. I wrote to the college and asked if I could sit my examinations, and they said yes. I then asked the man I was working for in the children's hospital, and he said no. By that time, I was sick of being someone's boy, so I sat them anyway. I was still a resident, but I started to look for a job.

There were so many fabulous places. I almost went to Chapel Hill in North Carolina, but the chief there, Frank Wilson, for whom I would have been happy to work, was probably going to New York. Roanoke was possibly the most beautiful city in the US, but to get there, one had to take a small commuter plane from Chicago, and I had a lot of international traveling to do. The climate in Albuquerque, New Mexico, was perfect, but there were too few people in the state to support a joint replacement surgeon. I really wanted to go to the US, but Professor Dewar offered me a job in Toronto General. There is always the sense that if one is given a job where one was taught, that is a singular honor. So I took the job. I do not think I was terribly popular with the men who were now my colleagues, but I really did not care.

CHAPTER 13

FELLOWSHIP TRAINING

As part of the deal in joining Toronto General, I had to go somewhere else for some subspecialized training, so I went to London. Mike Freeman, in the London Hospital in Whitechapel, was setting the world on fire with his ideas on knee replacement. I had met him at the Gordon Conferences, where I was speaking, so he knew about the work I was doing with fixation of implants to bone. He asked me to spend a year as his fellow. He never did anything with the technology I had because of patents and other things. I did not have the patents; it was my original boss that had it. That was the way of the world, and I never ever thought it should be different. I did the work, but without his support, I couldn't have done it. When you are young, you can always make money later.

The year I spent in London was exciting in many ways. Mike Freeman had an enormous waiting list, stretching out for years, as all he did was joint replacement. I was given Friday for my operating list. What that meant was if I got into trouble, I was on my own, as by Friday afternoon, every other surgeon had left London. I got into the habit of leaving the operating room and having a smoke and think. This became a lifelong pattern. If you are in trouble and you stay in the operating room, you get more and more desperate. If you leave and sit and think, the answer usually comes pretty quickly. On reentering the operating room, one has to rescrub and regown, so my nurses used to grade cases as a one-gown case, two-gown case, or for the really difficult ones, a three-gown case.

One interesting thing I did was go through the list and do the operations I had never done in training. One day, I remember I did three Lambrinudi procedures, which is an unusual and fairly difficult foot operation. The first took me some time because for part of it, the operating room nurses had to read the appropriate paragraph from my trusty Campbell's surgical textbook. The second was pretty good, and the third was a breeze. That is what we have always been told in orthopedics—see one, do one, teach one.

Mike Freeman thought I was nuts doing all these weird operations, but it stood me in good stead. When the boat people came to Canada after their escape from the fall of Vietnam, their incidence of old polio was huge. In the West, we had not really seen polio for so long. The older surgeons who knew what to do had retired, and the younger ones had no training, so with my experience in London, doing these weird operations, I could actually help these people.

London is about as close to the center of Europe as one can get. I therefore wanted to visit all the great joint replacement surgeons. That sounds like a tall order, but really it was not, as there were not that many. Even in the US, the numbers were small, like Mike Linebach in Florida, John Insall and Chit Ranawat in New York, and a few others. I was able to take time off to visit Europe because I had two fellows with me from the US who covered for me. One of them, Jeff Rubin, wanted to go to Scotland with me to see the Edinburgh Military Tattoo. I told him that was for tourists. He pointed out that by that time, I was a tourist.

One of the surgeons I visited was the great Robert Judet in Paris. He had been a major figure since the fifties. He had his own hospital in the Fifteenth Arrondissement in Paris. Being insouciant French, the men and women used to change into operating room garb in the same room. His anesthetists all looked like Catherine Deneuve. I kept asking him for a job. I would have been quite happy to live and work in Paris. He had this wonderful operating table, which was like another two assistants. The patient was tied to the table, which was controlled by two long-term employees. He would make an incision, shout something, and the hip would dislocate. He would cut the head off and shout again, and the femur would disappear. He would fix the socket and shout again, and the femur would magically appear. He would prepare that, put the implant in, and shout again; and the hip would go back in joint.

He would start off every operating list with three hip replacements, then he would say that we will have a crust of bread and a glass of wine.

Then we will really operate, and he really did. He was the expert on broken bones that had failed to heal, or rather that was one of his areas of expertise. So he got patients from all over Europe. He and an assistant were the original pioneers of repairing pelvic fractures, which no one had done before then. The volume of surgery was immense, and the skill was something to behold.

He was very amusing. The status of Britain had been on a long downslope, so he called all English-speaking surgeons American. "You Americans," he would say to me, "you are stupid. You pay $1.5 for a single suture. Me, I pay $1.5 for fifty meters of nylon fishing line." He would sew the hip patients up with this huge crochet hook, which he pushed through the skin, all the way through the tissues and out the other side. He would then hook his suture, pull it back, and tie it. He could close a hip incision with three sutures. It looked terrible, but I never saw any problems.

"You Americans, you are stupid, you pay taxes. Me, I never pay taxes." I was about to say—in typical Gallic fashion, but I am not sure that is correct—he bribed whoever was in charge of France. He once backed the wrong horse, and Giscard lost the election. They came after Judet and threatened to put him in jail. He was given stern instructions not to leave France. Judet, who had not left France for years, began to turn up at international meetings he had never been to before. He even came to Toronto, where he made a huge impression on the wives of the attendees.

He knew of some of the animal work I had been doing and was not impressed. "You Americans," he would say, "you are stupid. You spend all this money on dogs. Me, I operate on Frenchmen, and they pay me. Once I am sure it works, then I do two dogs."

He was one of the giants. I once saw him do a huge slash down the leg. I thought, *There goes the popliteal nerve.* He put his little finger into the lower end of the incision and pulled out the nerve, completely unharmed. Magic.

Maurice Müller in Bern in Switzerland was another famous, larger-than-life figure. He, with a group of Swiss surgeons, formed a society to study trauma. They called it the Association for Osteosynthesis, or AO for short. Osteosynthesis is the joining of bones, another way of saying fixing fractures. They, along with an engineer called Perrin, set about systemizing the hardware used for fractures. It certainly needed fixing. Some of it was so ludicrous it is hard to believe. For example, one British company cast screws. To *cast* means "to pour molten metal into a mold and let it harden."

No mold is completely smooth, so the resultant screw is rough. This does not matter if the screw is being put into wood, but if it is put into living bone, the bone will grow up around the rough areas on the screw, which makes it almost impossible to remove. I used to see hardware like this when I was a resident. We could not tell on an x-ray. If the screw was made in the US, it was machined and therefore smooth and could be taken out easily. If it was made in the UK, it was going to be a long day. It surely does not take a rocket scientist to see there might be a problem.

Another thing was the screw head. The metal used for fracture surgery is stainless steel, not the steel used for one's knife and fork, which is 314L. In surgery, we use 316L, although I could tell you a funny story about some implants I was asked to consult on from a country which shall be nameless. The implants were failing. I found that 316L was going into one end of the factory and 314L was coming out the other. Stainless is a pretty soft metal, which is easily deformed. The wood screws one buys are much harder. If the notch for the screwdriver is cruciform (what is called a Phillips head) or, even worse, a flat head or single groove, then all it takes is one slip of the screw driver and the metal will be deformed and the screwdriver will no longer hold the screw.

Elementary, my dear Watson, one would have thought. The Swiss began to use a hexagonal notch that gets a much better grip, and wonder of wonders, the problem of stripped heads went away. Actually, the Canadian Robertson head, which is square, is even better. Leda, an engineer I worked with on artificial hips, wanted to introduce this into surgery, and we did make some prototypes. But then she got married, and it was just too much work, and we eventually gave up. There were other things, such as if one squeezes two rough surfaces together, they are more stable. Think of compressing things after one uses glue. Methods of squeezing bones together were developed, and all sorts of other commonsense things. The problem is, how do you tell the world what you have done? The previous method was to tell the universities and let them teach it. That would have sort of worked in about fifty years or so, perhaps.

The genius of the AO group was to do something radically new. It was about as revolutionary as the printing press or YouTube.com. They set up teaching courses completely bypassing the universities. This was what I later became part of, which we called the Traveling Road Show. They brought surgeons in from all over the world to Switzerland and taught them and then sold them the equipment. They also took the show on the road.

They revolutionized fracture surgery. In terms of relieving human suffering and misery, they never got the recognition they should have, which was monumental. I once heard someone say that that group should have been given the Nobel Prize. I thought that was pretty stupid then, but now I think maybe that was a reasonable assessment of their contribution.

No one feels sorry for them, because being good Swiss, they monetized it. It was rumored that at one time Maurice was making a million dollars a day. I do not know if that was true, but I hope it was. He deserved it.

Maurice was a hard man. The rumor is that he went to England to see what Sir John Charnley, the English pioneer, was doing with this new hip replacement. He came back to Switzerland and told them that there was nothing in it. Two weeks later, the Müller hip joint was for sale. The stories about Maurice are legends. There was the time his wife broke her ankle heli-skiing. He was waiting for her at the bottom of the mountain. He held her hand and told her he would get the best surgeon in Switzerland to look after her. An hour later, when she was lying on the operating room table, the door banged open and Maurice came in, saying, "I am the best surgeon in Switzerland," which was probably correct.

There is the story told that the king of Saudi Arabia needed a new hip. He got in John Charnley from England. Charnley opened his hip, thought it was infected, so he stopped. The king woke up, was displeased to find the operation not done, so he said, "Get me the German." So Maurice came and did his hip. When the king asked how much, Maurice was reputed to have said, "In Switzerland, we ask for the patient's wage for one day." Considering all the oil money in the kingdom, in theory, belongs to the king, that would certainly have been a well-paid operation. History is silent on how much Maurice actually got.

Seth Greenwald told me this one, as he was a participant. Maurice was about to start the morning's operating list, but his assistant, Ganz, was late because his car had broken down, so Maurice needed an assistant. He looked around the operating room. There were a couple of seedy-looking Frenchmen, a scruffy Englishman, and Seth, who was an American engineer who was there to set up an information retrieval system for Maurice. He asked Seth to scrub. Half an hour later, Ganz came in apologizing. Maurice said, "Go away, Ganz, Professor Gruenwald will assist me." He would not let Ganz back in for a couple of weeks until Seth finally pointed out to him that while it was nice and he was learning a lot, that was not what he had been hired to do.

Seth said that for one case, Maurice forgot to put on his face mask. The nurses were afraid of him and would not tell him. Seth, ever the diplomat, said, "Professor, your mask has slipped." The answer was "I do not need the mask."

I liked Müller. Bern is one of the few places in the world where you can spend a week and no one talks to you. For a Swiss man therefore, I found Maurice quite friendly. I mean, it is hard to dislike a famous surgeon who shows a very junior visitor an x-ray and says "What the hell am I going to do with this case?" and means it.

CHAPTER 14

OTHER GREAT MEN

One of the other surgeons I wanted to see was Heinz Wagner. No one knew much about him, but there were rumors that he was something special. He lived and worked in a small town in Germany, not far from Nuremberg, so I flew into Nuremberg and got the train to Altdorf. I mean, I have been in trains in Europe all my life, so I thought nothing of it. A ticket taker came around, clipped my ticket, and told me something that clearly I did not understand. A young German got up from down the cabin, walked up to me, and told me the train would stop for half an hour at the next stop. He then walked back and sat down. When the train stopped, he got up again to get out with everyone else and asked me where I was going. When I told him Altdorf, he asked me why, because after all, that is a nowhere place in the middle of nowhere. When I told him I was going to visit Wagner, he knew I was an orthopedic surgeon because that would be the only reason anyone would go to Altdorf. Then something rather amazing happened. There are lots of nice people in this world, and this man, Dr. Dan, who himself is an orthopedic surgeon, is certainly one of them. He took me to his home, and I had supper with him and his wife, and then he drove me to Altdorf and made sure one of the residents looked after me. It is hard to forget a man like that.

Wagner was what the rumors said: he was different. I mean, I have good hands, Judet had good hands, Müller had good hands, but Wagner was different. I am sure a man who sculpts must feel the same when he looks at a Michelangelo statue or maybe a basketball player when he looks at LeBron. It would look as if he was slow, the wound would fall open, there was no bleeding, and the case was finished.

Before I go on with this adoration, I should tell you a bleeding story I got from Kris. Kris Keggi is the US surgeon who pioneered small incision surgery. It became all the rage after someone visited him, went home, and began a superb advertising program. Minimally invasive surgery became what every patient wanted. What it was, was minimal visualization surgery. It was eventually stopped by a couple of insurance companies because the complication rate in surgery done by non-subspecialists and even these was unacceptably high. I actually did a couple of cases with Kris. I could do it, but it was more difficult than my usual approach, so I never really adopted it. At its maniacal height, patients used to come in and ask for a minimally invasive approach. Kris told me he had thought about monetizing it, as after all, he was the one who developed it and had been using it and teaching it to Yale residents for thirty years, and all hip surgeons in the US knew about it. He thought of having the Keggi instruments, the Keggi hip, and the Keggi whatever; but then he thought the Keggi headaches, so he never did.

He is originally from Latvia, so he would go back once a year to teach and show modern surgery to the local surgeons. He was operating on some high-up Communist official. The anesthetist was behind a screen. There were a few Swedish surgeons there watching as well. So Kris, who is a pretty slick surgeon, opens the hip and rips the head out, and says to the observers, "Look, no bleeding." At this point, there is a movement behind the screen, and the anesthetist gets up. The patient had died. The anesthetist had hoped that the pain of the cut would somehow make him alive again.

Wagner operated in this very large room with four operating tables, where he worked at one and his residents at the other three. Even for Germany, the efficiency was astounding. If anyone got in trouble, he was there. The whole thing was a clean-air room. The patients would be anesthetized outside the room and pushed in through the screens. Overhead lights could not be used, so the room was surrounded with banks of Mercedes headlights controlled from a panel that looked like something from NASA. Harold, who served Wagner with whatever he needed, was a big man and not someone you would wish to cross. He had been a Flak (antiaircraft) gunner during the war. If Wagner was in trouble, he would shout Harold's name. Harold would sit down at the console, and every light in the room would swing around and concentrate on Wagner's incision.

Wagner could do things that no one else could do, which of course is a bit of a problem because other people would try his operations, not terribly successful in some cases. Nonetheless, many of his innovations were a very significant step forward.

I developed a technique several years later to take out implants. I was at a meeting fighting with him about something or other when he showed his version of my operation. It was so obviously superior to mine that I always did his version from then on.

One of the problems with Wagner was that he had very little follow-up. Everything works for a while, but the question is, how long? In joint replacement, for example, we are not interested in results with a less than two-year follow-up, which in practice is about five years. Five- or ten-year results are much better to evaluate an implant. One problem is that most implants have a ten-year life cycle before they are replaced by a newer version. Wagner knew about the case he had done from Altdorf and the few from Nuremberg, but most of his patients were sent to him by a religious organization, so they came from all over Mitteleuropa and never came back to see him.

He cannot defend himself now, so I will not tell other stories. If one knew the complications of his operations, he would tell you how to fix it, but if you did not, he would not. For many years, we disagreed over many things at many meetings, but I never lost my admiration for him. I would start every attack by saying that he was the greatest surgeon I had ever seen, that it was like watching God operate.

It was once when I was visiting Wagner that I met the man I most admired, Renato Bombelli. By this time, we had stopped doing hip realignment operations in North America, or at any rate, I had, as I felt I could and would eventually make artificial joints that would last forever. We were certainly not at that point when I met Bombelli. Artificial knees lasted seven to fourteen years only. The operations Bombelli and others were doing left the patients with their own tissues and did not give complete pain relief, but it could always be converted to an artificial joint later.

But it was not so much what he did as who he was that was so impressive. He worked in a small town called Busto Arsizio, about forty kilometers from Milan. He was the *primario*, or head surgeon, in the local hospital. They had rebuilt the hospital around him, but he would not move out of a very old operating room, in what was now the hospital garden. It was frankly medieval. The autoclave, the pressure cooker used to sterilize instruments, opened into the operating room, so the temperature soared every time it was opened, and the humidity was like a mist.

But he had his own nurses. He said if he moved into the new hospital, they would become the hospital's nurses. Because he had control when the operating list was finished, everybody went home. He therefore got through about five hips between 7.30 a.m. and 1:00 p.m. Everyone worked flat out and rotated. The girl who scrubbed for one case cleaned the floor for the next one. The changeover times were just long enough for an orderly to pull the sweat-soaked shirt off his back and bring him a small espresso, and then they were ready for the next.

Changeover times—that is, the time from when one case finishes and the next case begins—varies tremendously. University hospitals tend to be terrible. In Toronto, for example, one teaching hospital used to be able to do three joint replacement cases a day, whereas I could do six, or I could until the administration added ten minutes to the changeover time, which cut the number I could to five. I once, in a bravura performance, did six hip revisions in one day. This was for a group of visiting English surgeons. By the end of the fifth case, they were tired and went back to their hotel. We once had some time and motion students come up from Waterloo's engineering department to study the operating suite in my own hospital. The difference between the most efficient nursing team and the slowest was forty minutes. When you think that the average cost of an operating room is between forty dollars to eighty dollars per minute, that is significant.

Bombelli's insistence in keeping control of his own nurses was good because when the work was done, they all went home. In my case, I never had control of my nurses, so while the great girls who worked on my team were greased lightning, when my list finished, instead of going home, they had to go and assist in the operating rooms where the slower teams were still working. I always thought that was so unfair.

It was everything about Bombelli I admired. He was so calm and quiet and caring, and he loved the same woman till the day he died. His staff worshipped him. I was back in Busto Arsizio twenty years after I had last seen him, teaching revision surgery. When the *primario* found out I knew Bombelli, he phoned him. By that time, he was in his late eighties, but he came down and watched me revise a hip he had put in himself twenty years before. A couple of his old nurses were still there, so it was very emotional for them and for me.

Anytime I was near Italy, I tried to visit him. There were a lot of us North Americans who did—Pompey, who was the professor at Rice in Dayton, Ohio; Rick Santori from San Diego, who became the hip osteotomy expert in the US; Gianni Maistrelli from Toronto, who actually did his follow-ups for him. He asked me to translate his book on osteotomies. He said his English was good, and he had translated it himself, but he wanted it written in English English not Italian English. To do that, I used to fly to Milan from Toronto on Thursday night. I would stay on my own time and fly back Sunday afternoon. It took me about a month. Springer-Verlag, the German publishing house, paid travel expenses.

He told stories about the great Italian surgeons, like Scaglietti, the famous surgeon in the Rizzoli Institute in Bologna. He told me how he once was in a hurry, so in order to get into the operating room, he pushed the surgeon, the anesthetist, and the operating table with the patient on it out into the corridor. When I was a visiting professor at the Rizzoli, I told them that story. They would not confirm it. Funnily enough, the last patent I had, I shared with the professor in the Rizzoli. That is one of the most romantic hospitals in the world, set high above Bologna, looking out on the rolling hills of Tuscany.

CHAPTER 15

MY OWN MAN AT LAST

When I got back to Toronto, I was a staff surgeon at Toronto General. It sounds great, but being the most junior staff member leaves little to be desired. No one wants to do the amputations, and as we had a big vascular unit, there were lots of them, and that is the junior man's job, my job, until the next man was appointed about five or six years later. It was not that I could not do them, as I had after all worked with George Murdoch when I was a medical student; it is just that it is an admission of failure, that nothing else can be done. That is not the North American attitude. The only one case I remember was one very late night, I took a leg off at midthigh. The patient was very elderly and delirious, as so many were, because their dead limb was poisoning them. I could not saw through the bone. I was cursing the weak, underpowered saws and eventually picked up a chisel and gave it a whack. Nothing happened, but the chisel showed a big notch, so I realized there was metal in there. The patient had had a metal hip put in years ago, and the scar was so faint it could not be seen. And of course, he had no family to give a history, and he could not. People are always hearing horror stories about the wrong leg being cut off. It sounds terrible, but the reality, in some of these cases, is that it can be hard to tell which one is worse. If you are taking off one leg tonight then the patient lives, you will probably be taking off the other next week.

There are always limits in any health-care system. It is simply not possible to provide all things to all people. Even robbing selected Peter to pay for collective Paul has limits. There are not enough Peters. In any socialist medical system, access is limited by waiting lists, and surgical waiting lists are produced by reducing access to operating rooms. As the low man in the system, this was obvious. I was allowed one day of elective surgery during the winter and half a day during the summer. Fortunately, the operating room staff was just so good that they could change over a room in minutes, and I was pretty quick, so I did not starve. Besides, I still had lots of research to do, refining parameters. I supervised a very clever PhD student engineer, Dennis Bobyn, who did some superb work and remains very well-known to this day.

The first of the new ingrowth hips were manufactured, and I began to put them in. I then thought of a snag. I could reliably put them in, but I did not know how to take them out. We tried various methods. Ultrasound that produce microscopic vibrations and shock waves seemed the best way to go. If we could have locked the probe on tightly, this might have worked, but it would have required welding in the operating room. Welding machines are really not compatible with some of the gases the anesthetists use, and setting the patient and the room on fire did not seem a very viable option.

I tried to take implants out of animals with a nonlocked system via a chatter cup. The probe I was using was about the size of a roadside pneumatic drill. It was like the mad scientist in a horror movie. I could vaporize the animal, but the implant remained fixed to the bone. I still have not solved that problem. The only way to take an implant out is to physically cut it out.

We noticed that if a solid implant was fixed to the bone, the bone under the implant became thin or osteoporotic. Bob Pilliar and I coined the term *stress shielding* for this. This is one of the big problems with zero gravity in space. If an astronaut is out in space too long, his bones will become so thin and weak that he will not be able to come back to earth gravity. Currently, the people in the space station exercise against elastic resistance in an effort to slow down the bone loss. Why it should happen under a metal plate was initially unclear, as there are many forces involved, such as bending, torsion, etc. Eventually, we tracked it down to axial stiffness. Once we knew what the parameter was, we could vary it from producing total bone loss to no bone loss. This then let us calculate what gravity would be required to prevent bone loss in space. Everyone knows that space stations in the movies are built like a wheel. The reason for that is, when the wheel is spun, the centrifugal force will produce artificial gravity. We knew what that gravity had to be, and I think we took out a patent on it, so we could tell them how fast they had to spin their space station. We tried to sell that to NASA. They, unfortunately, had no interest in a full-size space station and were content, for some reason, with that pathetic little tin can in space.

Since the patent has long since expired, as this was work we did in the late '70s, I can tell you. It is about one-sixth earth gravity. So in theory, we could live on the moon without too many problems. I dreamed of space, but JFK was dead, and his dreams of space died with him. Oh well, maybe someday.

On more mundane matters, having worked with Mike Freeman, I was one of the few trained knee replacement surgeons in Canada, or the US, for that matter. So I could do things others could not. One salesman tried to sell me his company's version of an artificial knee. I explained to him what was wrong with his knee in terms of design. This was Larry Laswell, who was an American who had moved to Canada. He would not take no for an answer. He said, "If this is so wrong, why don't you come down to Memphis and tell my people what is wrong and how to fix it." I was not too busy, so we flew down the next day.

CHAPTER 16

THE START OF THE ROAD SHOW

Sometimes in life, you get lucky. The man running the knee division was Tim McTighe, who became a lifelong friend and was my best man at my last wedding. We still work together. He listened to what I had to say and said, "Sure, we can do that. Sign here." So I did, and he did, and my first joint was born. We modified it for the first year, but after that, it became one of the best-selling knees in the world for about ten years.

Of course, nothing sells itself, and very few people at that time knew how to put them in, so it was time for the Traveling Road Show, just as Maurice Müller and Charles Bechtol had pioneered. Inside America, I was teamed with Dick Laskin, a surgeon from New York, as the company was not certain how well a foreigner with a funny accent would be received in the US, which initially was the only market anyone cared about. Fairly rapidly, however, it became obvious that Europe and some parts of the Far East had the money to be able to afford this type of surgery, which initially was not cheap, and had surgeons capable of being trained to do it.

In those days, travel was fun. People used to get dressed up to fly. I had a further bonus. I was a pretty good foot surgeon and was actually one of the founding members of the American Foot Society, and one of my students did a lot of very good outcome research on foot surgery. She had been a Canadian class figure skater and could jump three feet vertical in high heels. She later became a doctor and is now a professor of obstetrics, a very impressive person.

I did most of the bunion surgery for the Air Canada's air hostesses. That is not as easy as it sounds. These girls had to be back at work in airplanes in high heels six weeks after surgery. That was certainly good for upgrades to first class and caviar. I know most people do not actually like caviar, so the air hostesses would give everyone a tiny teaspoonful only. When they had done that, I would ask for the tin, a spoon, and some ice-cold vodka. Forget the other rubbish they used to serve with it like chopped egg and onions.

Speaking in the US consisted of company-run meetings and hands-on sessions with plastic bones, which usually were held on Fridays so the surgeons could take a little time off with their significant other on the weekend. Some of the places were very nice, like the Barrier islands down the East Coast of the US. There were some exploratory trips to scope out countries to see which to concentrate on because no one knew. So a bunch of us went on the road to give talks to surgeons in various countries.

One of the first stops was the Philippines. That made sense, as half the nurses in the world come from the Philippines. Without the nursing schools there, Western medicine could not function. Every year, they turn out thousands of very well-trained, hardworking nurses. The other product from the Philippines are entertainers. Everywhere you go in the Far East, the band and the singers are from that country. A couple of US salesmen from Memphis, Bill and Glen, were with us. This was just after Marcos had been deposed. One of the Americans was bribing the customs officer to let the product come into the country. Something I have never heard of before or since happened. The custom's officer told Bill that that was too much bribe money and gave some back.

The Philippines, of course, had no money and could not afford the type of surgery and implants we were selling, so it was a couple of decades before we went back. I once had a patient from the Philippines. He had broken his hip as a very young man and would have been condemned to a lifetime on crutches. An American visitor heard of this, and the next time he visited, he brought a metal hip in his pocket. A surgeon there put it in, and the patient walked and worked on it for the next twenty-five years. When I saw him, the metal hip, which was never fitted in the first place because there are, of course, a range of sizes (and how could a nonsurgeon know which size?), had sunk down inside the femur and into the pelvis, such that I did the first extended trochanteric osteotomy to get it out. This was the operation that I devised, which Heinz Wagner did better. The fact that the patient had functioned on that hip for so long was a testament to the triumph of the human will.

The second place we went to was Hong Kong. I will never forget the Mandarin Hotel on the Kowloon side. The bellhop showed my wife and me into our room and opened the curtains. We were looking down on the stunning view of green waters of Hong Kong harbor, with the boats coming and going, and across the harbor, the stacked high-rises of Hong Kong proper. They have now put a boardwalk at the back of the hotel, so the view is no longer so spectacular. He then brought a pot of jasmine tea. I really did not think that life could get much better than that.

For a long time, medicine there or, at least, surgery had been run by Australian surgeons. The big problem was TB. There was of course no medicine in mainland China as Mao had destroyed that during his cultural revolution, so the incidence of TB in the people who escaped from China was huge. This problem had not been seen in the West since the discovery of antibiotics by Gerhard Dogmak and, by the 1940s, streptomycin and PAS were available to treat TB. People nowadays have no idea what a scourge TB was. My father told me that when he was young, men used to go about with their shirt neck open because they thought that somehow that would give them resistance to TB. There were all these despairing novels by Erich Maria Remarque, the man who wrote *All Quiet on the Western Front*, and others about bright young things having their last romances while they were dying in sanatoriums in Switzerland, as the mountain air might give them a few more months of life. When I was a medical student, a couple of the chest doctors who taught me had been reduced from running their own hospitals to a few beds in a general ward. The big problem in Hong Kong was spinal TB. This produces the photographs one sees of these horribly deformed and twisted people. A few of these were due to untreated scoliosis, but most were due to TB.

One Hong Kong surgeon had developed a method of fixing TB of the spine, which revolutionized this type of surgery, and I do mean that it was hugely significant. He could operate from the front of the neck. Before then, surgeons went in through the back because there is not that much there, as opposed to all the clockwork in the front of the neck. But the front of the neck is where the problem is.

Korea was the next stop. We were in the Shilla Hotel, which is one of these exquisite Far East hotels. I have been there so often they even know which room I prefer. Part of their gardens has the original city walls from the Chosŏn Dynasty. The room I was in overlooked a Buddhist university. The students were rioting, and clouds of tear gas were floating about. I asked the interpreter, Mrs. Kim, about the riots.

"Riots? Riots? This is South Korea. We don't have riots. Oh, that! That is just the students being noisy before their examinations."

We went from there to Beijing. We were picked up by the senior orthopedic surgeon in Beijing, Professor Woo. He had acquired a van, which already seemed crowded with people. Somehow we all managed to fit in with the luggage. A tight squeeze means something different in the East as opposed to the West. The poverty was astounding. On the drive in from the airport, I saw carts with solid wooden wheels; I mean, no spokes. I have seen these in paintings from medieval times. The roofs of the shanties passing as houses seemed to be largely rusty, corrugated iron sheets held down by big stones. The streets of Beijing were wide, incredibly dusty with dust blowing in from the Gobi Desert, with no trees and no cars.

We were having a banquet with some of the local surgeons. There were many dishes, some of which my wife had never seen before, like chicken feet. I mean, I can eat anything. On one trip in the Far East, I broke all three Western taboos. In Japan, I ate Black Beauty (horse) raw. I ate Willie (whale) raw. And finally, in Seoul, I ate Old Yeller (dog). So I had no problem with the chicken feet, but it was not exactly my favorite food. My wife could not eat them, so she dumped them on my plate, which I ate to be polite. The surgeon sitting beside her, seeing the empty plate, asked her if she liked it. She said she did, so he gave her a dozen more.

President Nixon had just been to China, and the rumor was they gave him mao-tai to drink. Mao-tai is possibly the worst alcoholic drink in the world. It makes cheap, poor quality Grappa look like an elegant, sophisticated drink. Nixon was reported to have drunk the stuff and smiled at Mao, to show he was not being fooled, and said, "Good drink." He was then reported to have turned to an aide and asked, "What is this awful shit?"

Glen, one of the salesmen, was giving a toast, so he gave part of the toast, raised his glass, and took a slug of mao-tai. Glen was a pretty big drinker, as we all were then, but he clutched his throat and could not carry on. Bill, the other salesman, had to finish the toast for him. Mao-tai was terrible. It was like a mixture of raw alcohol and fuel oil. They have improved it, so it is now relatively drinkable.

We lectured at the university hospital. Everyone was dressed in Mao suits, and they all looked the same. As they trooped in for the lecture the others and I were giving, Glen was shaking their hands. Professor Woo was looking sourly at this performance.

After one man passed, Dr. Woo said, "Do you realize you have just shaken hands with the gardener?"

The Chinese salesman who accompanied us from Hong Kong indicated that he could sell stuff but only to the military hospitals, as they were the ones who kept Mao in power. No one else could afford anything. He said that at least the university hospital was not too bad, as it had a tile floor. Most of the peripheral hospitals had earthen floors.

I never saw this myself. But one of my partners, John Cameron, said that once, he was operating in Indonesia, and the operating room where he was carrying out knee ligament surgery had an earthen floor. We drove out to the Great Wall. They were building a new highway on which the journey now takes about half an hour. This was being built by hundreds of army men with picks and shovels. There were no backhoes or bulldozers at all, nothing mechanized.

There was a huge divide in ages of the surgeons. The senior surgeons like Professor Woo spoke perfect English, and many of them had been educated in the US. Mao had closed the universities for ten years during the Cultural Revolution, so then there were no competent doctors, and then there were the very young doctors who had learned to speak English listening, totally illegally, to the *Voice of America* radio.

The Beijing airport was interesting. It was jammed with people simply standing around. Where they were going, I had no idea, as there were almost no planes lined up. They were not about to give way to anyone, so in order to get through to the ticketing desk, we had to form a flying wedge. Bill, who was the biggest, formed the *schwerpunkt*, or the tip of the wedge, with the men on the outside and the women in the middle. We then simply drove through the crowd.

The only other place I saw this happening was in the airport in New Delhi. It was equally crowded with people standing around. I actually think, however, that most were going somewhere. I heard this commotion beginning at the far side of this immense hall. As the commotion came closer, I saw bodies being thrown in the air. When the point of the wedge came rushing by, I saw it was a bunch of German farmers trying to make it to their plane on time.

We did not go back to China for about thirty years.

CHAPTER 17

OTHER INTERESTING CASES

After I had been in practice for some time, I began to collect some interesting cases. One of the reasons was that the hip I had developed could handle almost every problem. Another was that the sheer volume of arthritic joints I was doing produced oddities, and I was quite prepared to do things that had not been done before. Some were happenstance.

When the dictator Idi Amin threw the East African Asians out of Uganda, they went to the UK or Toronto. I was suddenly faced with a very large influx of patients needing knee replacement. The "Indian knee" is not for the faint of heart. The deformity is wondrous. The leg is very bowed—some through the knee itself and some from a bent tibia below the knee. The femur is subluxed laterally on top of the tibia. The bones are very small, so even the smallest artificial knees only just fit. The foot also has a characteristic incredible deformity, which must be taken into account in replacing the knee.

After a few cases in Toronto, which did not turn out well, these ladies were very dubious about surgery. Fortunately, the ones I had done did go well. All these ladies knew one another, as there were not very many Hindu temples at that time. I therefore started to get busloads of them coming to my clinic from the temple. They were led by Mrs. Siddi, as she spoke perfect English. She was a true lady, dignified and imperious. She would translate for the girls, as she called them.

"Now, now, girls, come along. Don't keep doctor waiting."

For years, she would shepherd the other women and look after them. I eventually replaced both of her knees. The last time I saw her, she looked old and tired, and I knew she was not long for this world. I was sorry to see the passing of such a great lady.

Partly as a result of that, I started to get other Asians from Africa, as after all, if they wanted this type of surgery, South Africa was the only place they could go in the whole of Africa. They were all very young girls with congenital hip dislocation. This meant that they limped. In that culture, if they limped, they would not be candidates for marriage, which was a tragedy. No marriage meant no babies, and no babies meant they might as well commit suttee now. So I replaced the hips in eighteen-year-olds, which was unheard of in those days.

They would come back fifteen or twenty years later. The hip I had put in had worn out. If I could redo it, that was good, and if not, then that was unfortunate but acceptable, as by that time, they had married and had children. A different way of looking at the world to be sure, but one I never quarreled with.

I got a case from Africa of a girl with a condition called osteogenesis imperfecta, which has many variants, but basically, the bones are so thin and of such poor quality that they break. And as children, they have so many fractures that they end up very deformed. This girl needed almost every long bone straightened out, which would involve multiple operations and would be extremely expensive. I could do it without payment, and I could talk the anesthetist into not billing, but the hospital would have to be paid. I happened to know the man who was running Toronto at that time, Paul Godfrey, so I contacted him and asked for money. He was no one's fool. He phoned Africa to make sure I was not being spun a story.

Satisfied with that, he contacted some men. I showed up at his office to make my pitch. There were three big old fat men sitting around a desk. They heard my story in silence, looked at one another, and said, "We will fund it." And they did. It took me about six months to straighten out everything. She was very astute. When she was interviewed by the media, just before going back to Africa, she charmed them, "Oh, Mr. Godfrey, you have made a young girl's dream come true."

Which I guess he had. Paul Godfrey, unfortunately, went off to run a sports media company, and since then, no one runs Toronto. Of the three men who funded her, one subsequently became my patient when I replaced his hip.

One of my anesthetists was very good at hypotensive anesthesia. He could bring the blood pressure very low to minimize the bleeding during surgery. As a consequence, I felt it safe to do Jehovah's Witnesses, who will not accept blood transfusions. No one else in Canada liked to do them, so I got them from all over, especially the Prairies. There was always a concern, but I never lost one. One boy who was a revision bled and bled, and I was worried he was going to die on the table. He dropped his hemoglobin from 120 to 40, but he was up walking the next day. What was interesting was that I did his other side a few months later with almost no blood loss.

When I was an intern, I worked for a doctor who looked after hemophiliacs. He said that the amount they bled depended on how they felt. If they felt good, they bled less. Whether this is true or not, I have no idea, but if it is, it explains the effect Rasputin had on the czar's children, who were hemophiliacs.

These Jehovah's Witnesses patients changed for the better the way we had been doing things. Prior to my doing them in bulk, we used to transfuse with blood if the hemoglobin dropped below 100. It became obvious that this was unnecessary, and unless there were special circumstances, the medical men now only transfuse if it is below 80.

After a decade or so, erythropoietin became available. This increases the number of red blood cells in the body. It was very expensive. The Witness temple was very clever. They negotiated with the company and got the stuff at half price for their congregation, which meant, of course, we used it on them all. Erythropoietin was the drug all the cyclists used, as well as someone else whose blood was at a pinch. It was no secret. Everyone in medicine and sports knew. The treatment of Lance Armstrong, the winner of the Tour de France on many occasions, by that sanctimonious prosecutor (I was about to use another word) was abominable. All the top cyclists at one time or another have been caught using unauthorized substances. It is impossible to compete at that level without some chemical help. What is the big deal? If I had carried on as an athlete, I would have had to use anabolic steroids, so what? There is all this junk science about the terrible side effects. Well, maybe, but most of it is about as real as roid rage, which is fantasy.

I also started to get dwarves, of which there are several different types. They call themselves the Little People and have a North American Society, which is very good because they can keep up with the most recent developments and often know more about their condition than the surgeons. My hip implant would go down to nine-millimeter diameter, which later we reduced to six millimeter for the Japanese, although I think less than six of these had actually been sold. To deal with these people, I developed an operation to expand the canal in tiny patients and, at the other end of the spectrum, an operation to reduce the size of the canal in people who measured more than twenty-one millimeters. The reason for that is that a twenty-three-millimeter diameter and up implant is so stiff that the patient can feel it inside the bone.

Chapter 18

THE LAND OF THE MORNING CALM

I always liked Koreans. They were tough, clever, hardworking people. I was there once a year for about twenty years, and it looked like I may be back in business there again soon. I once bought a fake Hermes scarf in Itaewon when that was the famous fake capital of the world. The lady I bought it from said that it was not fake; she made them for Hermes.

Speaking of fakes, I was once operating in Karachi. The surgeon who had invited me took me out boating in the Bay of Bengal with his brother, who owned a large powerboat. When I asked him what he did for a living, he said he was Ikea. As I knew, Ikea was Swedish, so I was a little puzzled. He explained that he did the manufacturing, and Ikea in Sweden made the labels.

Two of my fellows were Koreans, Young Bok Jung and Yoon Soo Park. They became the orthopedic leaders in Korea. The story of Park was interesting and showed the way things work there. Many of the hospitals are owned by the chaebols, the big industrial conglomerates.

When Samsung decided to build a new hospital for their employees, they went to America and hired the best-known Korean surgeons in America. In orthopedics, they hired Won Oh. His job was to find the best residents in Korea and send them off for further training. I got Dr. Park for two years, to teach him joint replacement. In Canada, when they build a new hospital, it comes in at least two years behind schedule and hugely over budget. The Samsung hospital was finished six months ahead of schedule and under budget, so they called Dr. Park to come home and get to work. It was and is a beautiful hospital. In the foyer at lunchtime, a concert pianist comes in and plays. It contains the presidential suite. If a visiting president requires hospitalization, that is where he goes. I saw around it. Even with nobody in it, there were still armed guards.

The first time I went there to operate, I knew none of the operating room nurses would speak English, so I took my own Korean nurse with me, who worked in my operating room. She had initially worked in Germany, where a lot of Korean nurses did, and then came to Canada. She was married to the only man who knew about as much poetry as I did. I was once quoting Gabriele D'Annunzio, and he not only had heard of him but he also dismissed him as a minor poet. I still remember lifting off from Toronto airport, flying into the sunshine at ten o'clock in the morning, drinking mimosas, and sitting beside one of the most beautiful women in the world with the lights glancing off her shining, long black hair.

We did a knee replacement in four hospitals that day. The last hospital was the National Police run by Dr. Ha. I was opening the knee. The nurse looked over my shoulder.

"Isn't that a right knee?"

"Yes, it is a right knee."

"Funny, all I have are the left knee instruments."

Seoul is not a small city, and it took them some time to find the instruments and get them to us. It so happened that the patient was a girl in her early twenties with a knee that had been smashed in a motor vehicle accident. It took about half an hour for me to rebuild the knee with local bone grafts, and by the time I had done that, we had the equipment.

My nurse and I were sitting outside the operating room waiting for transportation. We were exhausted. The girl's parents came by. The mother was dressed in those gorgeous traditional Korean robes. They said to my nurse that it was as if the gods came down to rescue their little girl. I felt like weeping as I write this; I still do. Somehow that made everything worthwhile. That girl got married and had children. The knee I put in her lasted twenty-three years. I know that because Professor Ha's son revised her when it finally wore out, and he told me about it.

That evening, we were so tired we did not want to go anywhere, so we simply ate at the restaurant on the top floor of the Shilla Hotel, where we were staying. Halfway through the meal, she put down her cutlery and said, "God, I hate the Far East!"

"What is wrong?"

"The goddamn waiter thinks I am a whore."

I had not really thought about it, but it made sense. In the early '80s, a beautiful young Korean woman with a Western man in an extremely expensive restaurant in an extremely expensive hotel, what else would she be? This is no longer true, but it sometimes was then.

On one other trip with that nurse, we were operating in Bangkok. When I am doing an operation to be videoed out to an audience, I need to be able to see a monitor so that I can see where my hands are; that way, I am not obscuring the visual field. There was only one cameraman with a tiny, little camera and a stepladder and an even smaller monitor, but he positioned it so I could see perfectly well. He was running around and did a very impressive job. The Thais asked the nurse if there was anything she would like to take back from Thailand.

"Yes," she said, "we will take the cameraman."

CHAPTER 19

THE LAND OF THE RISING SUN

Japan for me was always a magnificent dream, full of swords and blood and death and beautiful women in kimonos. A terrible place, like my homeland. They fought one another for four hundred years before the rise of the shogun.

There is the story told in Scotland, down on the borders. A man sat down to dinner, and his wife lifted the silver cover from his plate. On it were his spurs, which told him it was time to go raiding again. The only time the Japanese united was against the invasion of Kublai Khan. But they were spared, when the Kamikaze, the divine wind, destroyed Kublai's ships.

The first time I was in Japan was at a conference on bone growth. I had been interested in that for a long time. One big problem we had as trauma surgeons was that sometimes bone refuses to heal. Robert Judet in Paris worked out how to make them heal, but this needed an operation. The question was if they could be made to heal without an operation. I worked initially with a surgeon from Calgary who had developed an electromagnet, which we were fairly certain did work under some circumstances. Unfortunately, after years of living in Calgary with its weird climate, he retired and went to British Columbia and was never heard from again.

I began to work for 3M in that field. The person I worked most closely with was an Australian engineer. She was very good-looking, but what

I really remember was that she had the most beautifully cut pinstripe business suits I ever saw on a woman. My main interest at that time was redo spine fusions. This was when a spine fusion had been attempted and had failed.

A spine was fused when the disks had worn out and were producing unbearable pain. A fusion was simply to stop them from moving, by getting bone to grow around the disk. It was difficult to do the first time and exceedingly difficult the second. To do this, among other things, I ran an electrified coil of wire up amid the bone graft. I could have used an external power source, but that would have been very inconvenient for the patient, so we developed an implantable battery. I would stimulate one side of the spine and not the other so that I had control. I could measure the density of graft on an x-ray with a densitometer. It worked, but what was even more interesting was that when I used a blind coil, which was not attached to any power source, it also produced an effect. A weak one to be sure, but a real one, or I thought it was real. This produced some interesting thoughts. Some birds after all, I believe, migrate along the earth's magnetic lines guided by some sort of sensor in their nose. Maybe the blind coil in the patient was being activated by the person moving around, crossing magnetic lines of force. Who knows?

One of the bones that when broken heals poorly is the scaphoid in the wrist, so we developed an external battery-powered unit for that, which we were about to begin to sell when, for reasons I never knew, 3M closed down all that research and broke up the team. I was so busy with many other industrial contracts and irons in the fire at that time that I never really complained as much as I should have. In retrospect, what I should have done was buy their division from them, but they probably would not have sold it. Someday, I expect someone in 3M to discover our results and reactivate the program, but I've been waiting for more than thirty years for that to happen.

That happened with another research. A couple of engineers from a company whose name I do not even remember and I worked on an artificial disk for the neck. As it was a metal plastic composite, it must have been a plastics company. I thought it was pretty good. I had the technology to anchor it to the bone, and they had the technology to produce a composite that allowed it a little flexibility with no moving parts so that it passed the fatigue tests. It was certainly better than anything currently on the market. I still have one of them in my desk drawer. We thought we were about ready for clinical trials. When the company lawyers heard what we were going to do, they closed down everything and fired the two engineers. This was just after the disaster when Dow Corning was bankrupted by lawsuits fueled by the junk science of breast implants, so no nonmedical company wanted to be involved with anything medical.

I arrived in Kyoto. The first interesting thing I found was of the taxi driver absolutely refusing a tip. I had no idea why. The second was all these *maikos*, the girls in training to become geishas, walking around in their kimonos. I once actually attended a tea ceremony with a geisha. She played her shamisen and sang for me, or me and another thousand engineers. Ah well, better than nothing.

For some reason, I was also meeting with the Kyocera people, the huge Japanese ceramics company. Obviously, therefore, I was negotiating something to do with ceramics, but I forgot what it was. I think I was trying to source cheaper ceramic heads for a cheap and cheerful hip stem I had made. CeramTec in Germany would never give me a break because they had already cornered the market in the US. I wanted nothing to do with the French ceramics. Limoges may be very nice dinner plates, but the French were really not good at zirconium, and if they could not do zirc, I had no interest in their attempts at aluminum. I did not get very far with Kyocera either. I found out later that they had some interlocking interest in the German company, which possibly was why there was no competition.

In negotiating with that company, however, I did learn about the Japanese entertainment culture, and what I can say is that if a Western man ever wants a good time, Japan is the place to go. There are things called businessmen's clubs, where companies have tables. At the company table, the men sit around talking and drinking. The club supplies women who sit with the men, fill their liquor glasses, and talk to them. The women move every half hour to the next table. They are not prostitutes. Some of them are fabulous. I was once in a club somewhere in Japan where none of the women spoke English, so the mama-san sent out to find someone. They found a JAL air hostess who could speak very little English only as she was on domestic runs. So she sat with me the whole evening. The stress on her as she tried to make conversation was palpable, and I felt sorry for her, but I did like her.

There was a club in Fukuoka where I used to go when I was in that city. There was a woman there who called herself the Boomerang woman. She had worked at the club, got married but did not like being married, so she got divorced and came back to the club, like a Boomerang, as she put it. I asked the Boomerang woman to marry me at least twice. She refused. She said, "Been there, done that, got the T-shirt." The last time I was there, she did give me her perfumed fan. I still have it. In times of trouble, I used to open that fan, and I could feel her scent and visualize her. But alas, the scent disappeared many years ago, along with my youth, but I still dream of might-have-beens.

When I became a consultant for Johnson & Johnson, I took my new hip to Japan. I began to work with Hitoshi Matsuo, the product manager for hips. For the next twenty years or so, we crisscrossed Japan. I was always happy to come during sakura time, when the cherry blossoms come out. They last for such a short time that they symbolize how fleeting life is. With four hundred years of war, the young samurai died by the thousands, their brief lives gone like the cherry blossoms. To sit under the tree, drink sake, and make up a haiku is one of the moving things of life.

Once, I was in Hirosaki, where the last samurai battle occurred. The gardens of the old castle there have not only sakura trees but also magnolias, which bloom at the same time, which I have never seen anywhere else. Another time, I started with a meeting down south in Kyushu and went north for various meetings, following the sakura bloom. I then went to talk in Korea at Gyeongju, the old imperial city. There was a reservoir there, and they had planted a double row of sakura trees on the path all the way around the reservoir. It was just spectacular.

When I was a child, I read Kipling's poem about the Buddha at Kamakura.

> But when the morning prayer is prayed
> Think ere you go to strife or trade
> Is God in human image made
> No nearer than Kamakura.

Obviously, it affected Kipling. When I walked onto the plaza where the big Buddha sits, it had the same effect on me. There was a sense of reverence, a sense of awe, something different. I mean, I have seen hundreds of statues of Buddha, but nothing like this. It has never left me, and every time I go back, I get the same feeling.

The only other time I got that feeling was when I was a child and my father took me to the Glasgow Art Gallery. There is a painting there by

Salvador Dalí, *Christ of Saint John on the Cross*. I know Dalí was a bit of a con man, producing numbered editions of prints into the thousands, but the world wants to be deceived. Look at what people pay for paintings by that other famous Spanish painter who could produce two masterpieces a day. Even looking at Dalí's painting on my phone produces the same effect, that this man on the cross who died for our sins may be the son of God.

I was a guest speaker at the Japanese National Orthopedic Meeting in Yokohama. That was fun. One night, the company had organized a boat trip around Tokyo Bay. This was just after the movie *Titanic* had come out, which the Japanese girl interpreters all absolutely loved. They all wanted to do the bit where the girl stands at bow of the ship with her arms outspread. I would pick them up by the waist so that they could lean over the bow of this boat we were on and do the *Titanic* thing. The surgeon who had organized it was pretty small also, so I picked him up as well.

The American engineer Seth Greenwald was at that meeting. Seth and I used to go jogging at 6:00 a.m. I found an opening into the docks where the Japanese naval fleet was tied up, so we would be jogging past battleships. Seth was worried we would be shot, but I knew no Japanese man would be awake at 6:00 a.m., so we were quite safe.

I also used to host meetings for Japanese surgeons in my own hospital in Toronto. Dr. James Bono used to come up from the New England Baptist Hospital in Boston to chair the meeting. Matsuo-san and my favorite translator, Kodama-san, used to come. Kodama was so good she translated for the prime minister of Japan. When I am using a translator, I leave a bud in one ear so I have some idea if I am going too fast. Kodama always used to drink tea when she was working, and I could always tell if she was in trouble because I could hear her teacup rattling.

I only hit an artery once in doing a hip replacement. It was a girl who had a congenital hip dislocation. In other words, she had been born with the hip not in joint. She had had a pelvic osteotomy done in Iran. Since that operation was developed in Toronto by Bob Salter, it was called the Salter osteotomy and was frequently done. I had replaced the hip of many people who had had that done in childhood, and I did not anticipate any problems. Unfortunately, the main artery to the leg that we normally never see in hip surgery, in this case, was somehow stuck to the front of the pelvis because of her previous operation, and one of the retractors punctured it. It was immediately obvious that there was a problem. Fortunately, the professor James Waddell was in the next operating room, so I got him in for a look.

He went and phoned the vascular surgeon at his own hospital, and by the time I had gotten the hip in, the vascular surgeon had arrived and repaired the damage, which actually was worse than I had thought as the vein was also stuck down, and the retractor had punctured the vein as well.

Furthermore, I had lengthened the leg to match the other side, so the hole was bigger than a simple puncture. Fortunately, the vascular surgeon was able to save the day, and she healed with no repercussions at all. I did her other hip a couple of years later.

The only thing was that all this was captured on video with thirty Japanese orthopedic surgeons watching. James Bono covered for me, but the schadenfreude was palpable. One could almost hear them say, "Ah, so that is how you do a hip."

The other person in the traveling group in Japan was Humi Hirai, who for years was my minder. I like to have a minder in the Far East because nothing is intuitive. Humi was a tall girl, and when I first went to Japan, I could see her almost across Tokyo. The girls got taller year after year. I had noticed this before. The girls in London were a lot taller than the girls in Scotland. I also noticed it in the Czech Republic, that the girls got taller before the boys. Clearly, it had to do with feeding. Humi eventually became Kodama's translation relief. I have always loved Japanese gardens, so we spent time visiting them when we could, especially one in Kyushu and an interesting garden in Niigata. This was a Chinese garden given by Chou En-lai to Prime Minister Tanaka and was sited inside a Japanese garden, which made an interesting comparison.

The other things I liked were the small hotels outside the cities. There was one in particular I remember. It was sited on the coast, and when I went jogging in the morning along the road, there was a sign saying, Beware of Tsunamis. That hotel had a hot spring further up the mountain. To sit in the hot mineral water pool in the morning with the shoji screen doors wide open, looking out at the sun rising out of the ocean, with the whole thing framed in Japanese pines—some moments truly are magic.

CHAPTER 20

SOUTH AFRICA

I was in South Africa several times. I think it was maybe the first time I was there that we were driving up the road from Johannesburg to Pretoria. The salesman who was driving me pointed out that we were passing the main military hospital. I told him that I knew the Brigadier Etienne Hugo. I had known him in Toronto, when he worked for Ian Macnab. The salesman wheeled off the road, and we went up to visit.

Talking to the brigadier was interesting. I learned all sorts of things I never would have otherwise known. Take the Angolan Civil War, which I knew nothing about other than the fact that the Cubans were fighting. When the South African troops overran a hospital supposedly staffed by Cubans, the military were horrified at the primitive conditions with every patient infected. The brigadier was phoned, and he and his complete operating staff were flown up to clean the place up. The brigadier also broke the apartheid ban when he pointed out that he could not separate wounded soldiers from the same unit, and therefore, he had shared wards.

Speaking of Cubans, the government there has for years been telling the world about the wonderful health care they have there, available to all. When I was teaching joint replacement surgery, we only went to countries which could afford it, as it was expensive. All modern medicine is expensive. I therefore had a little difficulty believing that a bankrupt island like Cuba could have "modern health care" for no money. I was there on holiday, and one of my children got a red eye, so I had to take him to a local clinic or hospital. The doctor was nice, but when she threw open the medicine chest to look for drugs to treat him, there was effectively nothing—virtually no medications—and none was available anywhere else on the island.

Once, I was due to speak in South Africa and had been somewhere in Italy and was flying into Munich to get a connection to Frankfurt. There was a very severe thunderstorm when the plane came in to land. Getting thrown around the sky was a fairly apt description. That was one of the few times I thought we might not make it. It happened to me three times before. Once, I was flying into Madrid. The pilot put the plane into a power dive. I knew that when he tried to pull out, the wings would come off. It was, after all, a commercial plane, not a fighter plane. I was amazed at how calm all the other passengers and I were. We just sat there. No one screamed. All I had was a vague sense of regret of things not done. And then he pulled out, and the wings stayed on. Thank God for Boeing.

The second time was when I was landing at Funchal in the Azores, in the middle of a rainstorm. The runway has been cut into the side of a cliff. It ends by vanishing over a drop of many hundred feet into the ocean. I could see out the window as the plane landed. I could see the cliff edge approaching. I knew we were going to go over, and again I felt absolutely fatalistic. I did not know I was so brave. The plane stopped with its nose over the edge.

The third time was landing in Gibraltar. I was sitting at the window, but as the plane came down, all I could see was the ocean. There was no runway. And then we touched down, and I still could not see the runway, only the ocean. It was so narrow that it could not be seen from the inside of the plane.

At Munich, we were delayed for about three hours until the storm passed over, and we could take off. I did not see how I could possibly make the connection, so I spoke to the stewardess. She said there were others on my plane making the same connection, and if I did not have checked baggage, I could make it. I do not think I have ever flown on a plane on my own with checked baggage.

The efficiency of Lufthansa may be legendary, but this was above and beyond. When the plane stopped at the gate, the stewardess had the four passengers trying to make the connection lined up. There were stairs waiting. We were bundled off and onto a jeep that drove to the end of the runway, where more stairs were waiting for us to board the plane for South

Africa. The stewardess had closed the door, and the plane was taking off before we got into our seats. Absolutely magnificent.

The South African Orthopedic Association was holding its annual meeting in Namibia, shortly after that country became independent, and I was a guest speaker. The main, or perhaps the only orthopedic surgeon in Namibia, was a Scandinavian who saw the world differently than most people. One of his pastimes was to sit on his front porch in the evening and shoot out the streetlights with his trusty .45, as they call these things in South Africa.

He was famous for an episode at a nightclub in Johannesburg. He asked the pianist to play him a tune. The pianist refused. He took out his trusty .45 and put a couple of bullets into the ceiling. His friends managed to get him out. On the way down the stairs, they met the police running up. The doctor said to them, "Be careful. There is a maniac up there with a gun."

There are other stories, including the time he stole the fighter plane, but perhaps that is a little far-fetched, although I have been assured by several people that it was true. The only one I know for sure is because I was with him. We were walking down the street in Windhoek during rush hour. Now rush hour in Windhoek is not exactly rush hour in Toronto, which has the worst commute in the world, but it was still quite busy. The doctor spotted an UNTAG (UN) officer. The United Nations were there in force. This soldier was from Libya or somewhere. The doctor pulled a certificate out of his pocket and showed it to the UNTAG man. He claimed to be a senior officer in the South African Command and demanded the right to inspect the UNTAG man's weapon, which he was given, as he sounded so authoritative. He cracked open the pistol. "Filthy, absolutely filthy. How can you carry a weapon like this? See to it!" And he spilled all the bullets into the gutter. He gave the man back his gun, and we walked off. The last I saw was the man on his hands and knees rescuing his bullets amid the traffic.

That was a good meeting. At one official dinner, the group drank every bottle of red wine in Windhoek. The stories told at that meeting were often hilarious, but I am not sure they would be appreciated by nonmedical audiences. I had to leave before the meeting was finished because I was scheduled to talk somewhere else.

The last time I was back in South Africa, the meeting was held in a game farm. Again, I had to leave early as I was scheduled somewhere else.

The drive back over the veld was terrifying. The vehicle was open, with no seat belts. It was dusk, and the driver was in a hurry as I was late for the plane, and there did not seem to be any speed limits. There were animals leaping across the unfenced road. There were no Stop signs that I saw at intersections and certainly no lights. In fact, there were no lights at all. At each intersection, there were crowds of people standing around wearing dark clothes, who blended in with the dusk. On that two-hour journey, I saw the bodies lying on the road of at least two pedestrians who had been hit and killed. I was exceedingly happy to see the lights of Johannesburg airport come up.

One other story I should tell was of one of my great nurses, Teresa Mapalan. She was Xhosa, I think, but I never really asked. She arrived in Saskatchewan in Canada because they were recruiting nurses in South Africa. They lured her with a photograph of a green verdant valley, so totally unlike the high veld that she agreed to come. When she got there, she found there was one small green valley in the whole of Saskatchewan; the rest was a flat prairie that went on forever.

She ended up in the orthopedic hospital, running the infected ward, which was a six-bed unit set up by James Bateman. This was 1978, and the treatment of infected joints was in its infancy, so when it became known that I would look after infected joints, I got swamped, ending up with a large number of infected cases. What I mainly did was take all the hardware out and wash everything out for a few days after cleaning the joint up. In my main hospital, the nurses could keep the irrigation system going for about twenty-four hours. Teresa and her ramrod, Zeda Webster, could keep it going for a week or longer. After doing an infected case, it is better to let the operating room air change for a long time before the next clean case is done, so I used to do these cases on Friday afternoon. We did cases most Fridays for about fifteen years. By that time, others felt they could handle their own cases. The operating room nurses called it the Pus Emporium.

Whether or not they were scheduled to work, one of these two women would always wait for these patients to leave the recovery room and get them settled in the infected unit. We were endlessly patient. The length of hospitalization did not matter, and I would reoperate as necessary, so there really was not a single case that I remember that we did not get cleaned up eventually. That is not to say that everyone got a joint back in again. Some men, fed up with the pain of repeated surgery and relapsed infections, were happy to give up and live with no joint. All women wanted a joint back in again. I think there were very few amputations, probably less than five in all that time.

There were however some strange cases. There was one man who would come in with strange abscesses. We would clean them up, and he would go home but come back a few weeks later with more abscess. We tested him for immune disorders but could not find anything. Teresa eventually spoke to all the infectious disease doctors at the university, and one recognized the patient. He suggested searching his room, which we did. We found the syringe and needles. He had been injecting himself with his own feces. There are some really strange psychopathologies out there.

I had another secret weapon in my arsenal. There was a retired professor of bacteriology from the University of Toronto who used to come in. I think the hospital paid him a tiny stipend, so it was not for money he showed up. He would have tea with Teresa and Zeda and look at the laboratory data. He would then recommend which drugs to use. He was enormously useful.

As Ontario slipped further and further into debt, increasing cuts were made, and my infected unit closed. Techniques had changed in any case. Teresa eventually retired and moved to Cape Town, where, unfortunately, she developed breast cancer, which was inoperable. She is gone now. I feel privileged to have known a great lady.

CHAPTER 21

AUSTRALIA

I was there often enough that I knew how to get there and back in the same day. Because there are now lie flat seats, I can tell you the secret because you do not need to know it anymore. You fly to LAX and catch a 747, which leaves at about midnight going to Sydney. It has to be a 747, and you have to have a window seat in the upper deck. The reason for that is that there are luggage compartments on the side, so if you have the window seat, you can lie flat. You then have a couple of doubles of your fancy, pop a long-acting sleeping pill, and pass out. You wake up as you are coming into Sydney at about midnight Australian time, take a short-acting sleeping pill, and sleep the night. The next day, you give your three or four talks and catch the same plane back at 3:00 p.m. the same day.

Make sure you do not forget to pack your passport as Seth Greenwald did once. He turned up at the immigration desk with no passport. The custom's man was questioning him, "Do you have a criminal record?"

"I did not know that was still required."

As Seth said, it is a mistake to get funny with an Australian immigration man.

The first time I was in Australia was when I was talking at their National Orthopedic Meeting. The one thing I learned was not to take a train full of young Australian orthopedic surgeons and residents going up to wine country. Going up was fine, but the way back was not so glamorous. They had the depressing habit of having drunk so much that they would fall down inside a locked train washroom and not be able to get up. That was OK for the men, as urinating out a moving train door is not an insurmountable problem, but unfortunately, I had a wife with me.

I soon got to know Bruce Shepherd. He was a force of nature. The doctors there were having a dispute with the government which, as I understand it, was trying to do a Canada on them—that is, to make private practice illegal, as it is in Cuba, Canada, and that other bastion of freedom, North Korea.

Doctors are not very good at going on strike. It goes against their nature. Fortunately, Australia still had enough private, nongovernment hospitals that they could operate on their patients outside the state system. Bruce Shepherd kept them on strike for seven years, until the government caved in and stopped their efforts to make private medicine illegal. During that time, the government tried to break them by bringing in doctors from all over the world to staff the government hospitals.

The Australian surgeons were all pretty good, so I don't remember any funny disasters. I do remember, however, doing a knee replacement in some smaller town. The surgeon there was talking during the operation to his anesthetist about hunting. He indicated that it was not safe to hunt feral pigs with a regular rifle, and he always preferred an American military assault rifle.

There was one story that one of my Australian fellows, Dr. Solomon, apparently told about me. I was driving him up to our cottage in ski country when the windshield wiper broke. This was on a very fast three-lane highway, which was jammed with people going north on a late Friday afternoon. It had been snowing, so the traffic was kicking up a huge amount of slush. I was driving a big old Cadillac, so it was difficult to get my arm far enough out of the side window to wipe the debris off the windshield. It was not possible to stop, so I had to keep going until the next turnoff, which seemed like twenty miles away. I made it, but it was a little hairy.

One interesting thing was that we found out that it was currently easier to manufacture in Australia than anywhere else. How long that will last before some government steps in, I do not know. It was President Reagan who said that the most terrifying words anyone could hear is that "we are from the government, and we are here to help you."

A funny thing occurred when I visited Canberra. The company had organized a meeting for me to give a talk and a demonstration. Surgeons had promised to attend, so I drove down from Sydney. An elaborate buffet was laid out, but only one surgeon showed up. We waited for a while, but no one else showed, so I simply showed him what I was doing and left. What I found out later was that he was the senior surgeon, and because his colleagues had embarrassed him, he bought the knee system for his whole department, so financially, that evening alone was worth a trip to Australia.

That happened to me once in the UK, so after that, I never agreed to attend a company-sponsored meeting in either of these countries. I would only go to meetings sponsored by their national body.

CHAPTER 22

EUROPE

Europe for me was always a Disney-like, enchanted kingdom. As a student, I wandered around, and when I was a fellow in London, I visited some of the greatest surgeons in the world. Almost anywhere I went, I found something magical. I got off the train once in Aachen. I cannot remember why, but I went to the little local museum. There was a magnificent painting I had never heard of. It was *The Descent of the Damned into Hell*; I want to say by Rousseau, but I am not sure. Similarly, when I was in Augsburg, I found the Fuggerei, a sort of village within a village set up by the Fugger bankers for their employees. And Italy of course. There are still hilltop towns I want to see, including Orvieto and Perugia.

I operated a lot in Italy. That was really have knife, will travel. There were constantly courses all over Italy. For a while, we ran courses in the Danieli Hotel on the waterfront in Venice, just beside Piazza San Marco. That was an interesting course because live surgery was done by one of my oldest friends, Luca Marega. He operated in his own hospital in Brescia. We had two-way voice, so I could speak to him from Venice during the operation. He once had a very difficult case. Fortunately, there were radically new design implants available, but they were so new he had never even seen them. He was such a technically good surgeon that, sitting in Venice, I was able to talk him through the preparation and insertion of the device.

Luca used to visit me in Toronto frequently when he started. He ignored the usual way of doing things in Italy, where one is a slave until middle age and then one becomes the chief and does not do much anymore. Luca went straight into private practice. This made him hugely unpopular with the other medical people, but he was so good that patients came to see him anyway. He used to take part in these 100K foot races, especially the famous race over the Apennines, which is run overnight. He gradually became popular as a lecturer, as he was almost Germanic in his precision. Eventually, he did more lecturing on my hip in Europe than I did, which by that time suited me. We had fairly similar tastes. One of my kids had a birthday while he was visiting me, so we went out to celebrate. After, we went to see the new movie *Muppet Treasure Island*, which I thought was one of the best movies ever made. Luca took a pirated copy back for his own children. Outside the Far East, Toronto is one of the pirated movie capitals.

Spain was another country I was always happy to visit for courses or as a visiting professor, from Teruel in the mountains to Malaga in the south. When I was a boy, I visited the Alhambra in Granada. I have a computer-generated print of it hanging opposite me as I write this. It was a tragic story. I replaced the hips of a husband and wife who were immigrants from Romania. I would recheck them every second year or so. They came in for their sixteen-year checkup, and everything was fine. Their daughter, who accompanied them, was making a name for herself as an artist. She was going to Paris in a few days to paint for six months. She complained of some aching in her hip. Normally, I would have done nothing, but because she was going away, and there might be insurance problems, I x-rayed her hip.

It was awful. She was absolutely riddled with secondary tumors from breast cancer she knew nothing about. The ache she had in her hip was because the holes in the bone carved out by the tumor were getting so large that her femur was about to break. This was the first symptom she had had, and she was so far gone that no treatment was even remotely possible.

It was not easy to tell a young woman who thought she was in the flower of life and whose career was just opening up and who was about to fulfill her childhood dream of going to paint in the City of Lights that she would be dead within a few months. She was very brave. She neither wept nor complained. The only thing she asked was if I could fix her so that she could go to Paris, even if only for a short time.

To do that, she would have to have metal rods put down the inside of both her femurs to stop them from breaking. I did not have that equipment in my hospital. We have a state system in Canada, which moves at the speed of a glacier. So I phoned the cancer hospital and would not get off the phone until I spoke to the surgeon who did that type of surgery. I called in all my favors and got her nailed that day. She went off to Paris where she painted for three weeks before she came home to die. She gave me a print of her recent work, which I will keep forever.

Her brother, who was also an artist, was distraught. He could not sleep. He tried to fill every moment with activity, so he did something which people said was impossible. He produced a computer-generated picture of the repeating ceiling of the Alhambra. He gave me one of these pictures. I know nothing about it, but I know he did win awards for it.

I had friends everywhere in Europe. One of my friends was a surgeon in Norway. I always thought he was a little crazy. He would disappear periodically. I eventually found out he was going to Afghanistan. This was when the Russians were there, and it was all-out war. He was operating on the wounded Mujahideen. He and I and a surgeon from Belfast did a trial of a new hip. I changed the geometry a little to see if these changes made any difference. They did not, but without doing the trial with large numbers of patients with a long follow-up, who would know?

They had a very strange system in Norway. The doctor could only work forty hours a week. If he worked more, he had to take time off next week. The system in Sweden was even more odd. It reminded one of Communism, when the government pretended to pay the workers, so the workers pretended to work. I am sure it has changed now, so I shouldn't laugh at it too much, but to see good surgeons do almost no surgery was a little depressing. The workweek began on Tuesday and finished on Thursday afternoon. I forget how many sick days there were, but I am sure they worked a few days more than they were off sick.

I do not want to sound too disapproving. The Swedish system meant that patients were allowed to go to their local hospital only. They could not shop around. This meant that long-term follow-up studies were possible. For example, the only good long-term study I ever heard of on the results of ankle fractures was done in Sweden, as the patients were followed up for thirty years. There are all sorts of junk science out there as follow-ups are too short, and numbers are too small.

Alf Nachemson, the famous surgeon from Gothenburg, gave a talk once that I never forgot. He said that if with an operation you cannot beat 70 percent good results, do not do the operation.

In one trip, I did a knee replacement in three countries. It was the Tricon knee. It was the most expensive knee on the market in Finland, the cheapest in Sweden, and in the middle of the pack in Norway. The meeting in Finland was interesting. It was at the Hannola Institute, where I did a couple of knees. I spent the evening with the Finnish surgeons and found that the old joke was not a joke. The story was that a Swede and a Finn were having a drink. They had the first drink. The Swede, being a Swede, said *skoll*. The Finn, being a Finn, said nothing. They had a second drink. The Swede, being a Swede, said *skoll*. The Finn, being a Finn, said nothing. They had a third drink. The Swede, being a Swede, lifted his glass to toast. The Finn hammered on the table and said, "Are we here for drinking or for conversation?"

We did talk about Karelia, because I knew that Von Mannerheim had sailed from Glasgow to command the Finns during the Winter War. I had a patient in Canada who had fought in that war. He had a large hole in the bone below the knee, which made replacement difficult. It was a bullet wound. He had been shot by a Russian female sniper, but he said he killed her anyway. The Finns really want Karelia back some day.

Most of the time, these were quick in/out meeting for me as I had a large practice in Toronto. Sometimes the places were so exotic that I lingered. Tenerife was one such place. It is a Spanish island off the coast of Africa, which is basically a volcano, but the climate is superb. We had a pretty big course there with many old friends participating, including Henrik Malchau from Gothenburg. He was the man who started the Swedish Hip Registry, where they tried to register every hip replacement done in Sweden so that it would be possible to tell which designs were failing. No one thought it could be done, as getting surgeons to complete more paperwork when they were already overloaded with it would be like herding cats. Sweden is run by a very socialist government, but even so, that registry was a milestone, and all other countries are trying to copy it, the best currently being the Australian registry. There were all sorts of things wrong with it, and the data was extremely crude. But nonetheless, it was a major accomplishment, and as far as I know, Henrik still owns it. Eventually, he got tired of being a good socialist and immigrated to New York.

What makes Tenerife of interest to medical people was their incredible handling of the air disaster. The senior surgeon told me how they accomplished it. Two 747s full of tourists collided on the runway. Fortunately, they did not catch fire, but there were a very large number of casualties. It was a Saturday afternoon, and the hospital had minimal staff on duty, so it was a recipe for disaster.

As luck would have it, there was a very important soccer match on TV, and Spain is soccer mad, so everyone on the island was watching. The surgeon in charge managed to interrupt the TV show to announce the disaster and that all hospital staff had to report immediately, along with all medical doctors, nurses, and blood donors on the island. It was absolute textbook handling of the disaster, and the whole world was extremely impressed.

One other interesting place to hold a meeting was Sardinia, where I had been previously when I was an assistant resident, along with my boss, the pathologist. It was a nice meeting, but what happened after was even more interesting. Professor Veluti invited some of us to visit his cottage on an adjacent island, San Pietro, where the tuna killing was about to begin. Tuna is very important to the Japanese.

I was once flying from Toronto to Tokyo. The man sitting beside me was Japanese, so we got to talking. I found he lived in Newfoundland and was a tuna buyer. He had bought a freshly caught tuna that morning in Newfoundland, had it in a body bag in the hold, and would have it in the fish market in Ginza within an hour of the plane landing in Japan. He told me one fish would make him a very large profit.

Tuna apparently swim along trails, much like caribou, and one of these trails was off the coast of San Pietro. The fishermen put up huge curtain nets to direct the tuna into a large net chamber called the Killing Room. When they think the run is over for the year, they kill them all in one day. I was there that day when they brought the tuna up. There were thirty-two of them and one swordfish. They were about the size of a man with an average weight of 130 lbs. One Japanese man bought them all. They told me they would be in Rome that night and Tokyo the next day. It was possible to buy a house on San Pietro for the cost of one tuna.

CHAPTER 23

THE MAN-MACHINE INTERFACE

The first artificial joint I was involved in was a hip replacement, using the technology we had developed to fix it in place. I soon realized that while I could put it in and the fixation was solid, I did not know how to take it out. As a boy, I was taught that "as sure as sparks fly upward, man was born to sorrow," so I always anticipated that whatever I put in, someday I would have to take out. It was not, as the great Tom Lehrer sang about rockets, "Once it goes up, who cares where it comes down / That's not my business says Wernher Von Braun."

Taking implants out was very much my business. I was then involved in a knee replacement. They worked reasonably well, but there were still problems with the kneecap (patella). All this work had to be done on humans, as there was no animal model. We therefore proceeded very slowly and cautiously. First, I showed that with the current knee design we had, patients were better with a kneecap replacement than just leaving the native kneecap alone. I then made a replacement that would cover the whole surface of the kneecap because it made sense that if it was completely covered, it could not be painful. That was wrong. It made no difference whether it was completely covered or not.

That actually was predictable, because forever, orthopedic surgeons have had to face young girls with painful kneecaps, and no one could find anything wrong. It was only years later that my partner John Cameron and

I realized that the problem was not the knee. It was the bone below the knee that was twisted. The knee itself was normal.

He came across the problem because he ran the University of Toronto sports clinic, and he kept seeing these girls with knee problems whose knees seemed normal. They mostly had the same story. They were athletic girls who had had a minor knee injury, but which never got better.

As we say in orthopedics, when I had done two hundred knee replacements, I thought I knew a lot. When I had done one thousand, I thought I was beginning to understand it. Now that I have done five thousand, I think maybe I know a bit about it. It certainly took more than five hundred cases before I began to have an idea as to the solution to the kneecap problem. In some knees, I could not make the foot face the front. If I used a fixed axis hinge, I could, but if not, as soon as I let go of the knee, the leg would turn out and the kneecap would dislocate. Eventually, it became clear it had nothing to do with the kneecap as such; it was a tracking issue.

Once we realized that it was the tibia that was twisted and the knee was normal, the solution was obvious. If the bone was twisted, then divide the bone and untwist it. The problem went away, and it was no longer necessary to replace the kneecap. Kneecaps do need to be replaced if the problem is isolated to the kneecap alone, which is pretty uncommon. My partner and I did more isolated kneecap replacements than almost anyone else in North America, and between us, we did about fifty cases in forty years.

Kneecaps are still replaced in the US because of the infamous trial lawyers. One of my friends, a New York surgeon, was defending another doctor involved in a lawsuit. The patient was not happy with the knee, and they had found someone to say that it was because the kneecap had not been replaced. The surgeon was pointing out that this was not necessary. During cross-examination, the plaintiff's lawyer nailed him.

"How would you bill for this operation?"

"For a total knee replacement."

"But you only did two-thirds of the operation? How can you justify that?"

Well, the jury believed the lawyer, so now almost all Americans end up with an unnecessary patellar replacement. Sometimes you cannot win.

The next endeavor was to develop half knees. One of the problems with the early knees was that we could not guarantee full knee bend after a knee replacement. Now we pretty well can. With a half knee, almost all patients get full knee bend. Full knee bend is only really important to plumbers, who have to get under a sink. I developed a couple of very nice half, or unicompartmental, knees as we called them. The problem is twofold. The first is that it looks easy, but in fact, it is technically difficult to put in properly, more so than a complete knee replacement, and it is fairly sensitive to being put in properly. I am sure there are some things you can stick in any old way, and it will sort of work, but not a uni knee.

The second is selection. It looks common, but in reality, there are not that many knees where the problem is one side and one side only. It may look that way on early x-rays, but usually it is not. Due to a combination of these factors, the early failure rate for unis was about 4 to 8 percent in the first two years, as opposed to about zero for complete knees, so unis fell out of fashion. Like many things, it was not the thing itself that was the problem, and some day, maybe it will come back. I liked it because I could put one in, in about twenty minutes as opposed to about forty minutes for a complete knee. And this is actually significant.

I was once operating in Jakarta. A well-known uni knee surgeon had been visiting about six months previously. He had done six cases, and I revised one of them, so the Indonesians were not impressed.

In the early '70s, I did a disgusting experiment. I was pretty sure of the answer before I did it, but being pretty sure is not enough. I made a big incision in rabbits and contaminated the incision. Half, I sewed up immediately, and the other half I left open for an hour and then sewed up. There were no infections in the ones I sewed up immediately, and the ones I delayed all got infected. So do not let anyone tell you that speed is irrelevant. That sounds a little extreme, so I should tell you about the world's fastest surgeon.

His name was Robert Liston, and I think he was an Edinburgh man working in London. His specialty was amputations. This really was about what all surgeons did from the time of the fall of the Roman Empire until Ambroise Paré, the French battle surgeon, born in 1510 in Laval in France, who introduced effectively modern surgery. Liston developed a special knife that bears his name, and I have actually seen a Liston knife. The rumor is that Jack the Ripper, the London serial killer, used a Liston knife. They used to do a midthigh amputation without anesthetic, and if you were slow, the patient bled to death or died of shock. Liston could take a leg off in about ninety seconds. He used to ask onlookers to time him.

One day, he was doing one of his amputations. He cut with such speed and power that an onlooker who was standing close by thought that he was going to be cut and was so frightened he dropped dead of a heart attack. His assistant was holding the leg with both hands with his fingers spread wide, and by accident, Liston cut off three of them, so his assistant died shortly after from sepsis, as there were no antibiotics then. The patient of course died. This was well-known by surgeons as the only case in the world's history with a 300 percent mortality.

One unusual thing I developed was an implant for painful flat feet. For a long time, I was interested in feet, especially the hind foot, as it was so little understood. For example, I knew that most of the terrible flat feet one sees on middle-aged ladies, when one is walking down the street, were due to a tendon rupture in the hind foot. Usually, when a tendon ruptures, the patient is immediately aware that something has happened, but I saw this immediate recognition only twice in very clever women, who knew something had happened but did not know what.

I got some of Professor Medley's engineering students at Waterloo to look at that for me. We eventually came to understand it, and the students wrote their thesis on it. The cascade of events was complicated, so I won't bother explaining it here. Once you know what the problem was, then it was not too difficult to devise a fix for it, and so I did. One of the things I did was make a mobile spacer with which I could jack open the outside of the foot to push the heel round, which corrects a flat foot. A surgeon I knew in the US made them for me in a little factory he owned.

This would be totally impossible today, but this was before the useless FDA, which I think began to regulate orthopedic implants in 1979, and even the more useless Canadian Health Protection Agency. I only did about twenty of them, and they worked pretty well. I had a professional male figure skater do his big jumps on one, and it lasted him about twenty years. This was a very small market, and there was just too much else going on, and I could only work sixteen hours a day. So I gradually lost interest in feet as there never was enough operating time, and I had other implants I had to design and test or wanted to test.

Chapter 24

CYBORGS

The early successes of artificial joints were so spectacular that the demand for them went through the ceiling. Patients previously had been condemned to a life of wheelchair misery and early death due to boredom and inactivity. After all, if you are in constant pain and cannot do anything, what is the point of life? Now they could return to things they had not been able to do for years. They always kept pushing to do more. Initially, we were afraid that if they did too much, the bearing would come loose or wear out. As indeed they did. The first knees I put in were wearing out in seven to ten years, whereas now the materials are so good that we tell the patients twenty-five to thirty years.

For years, I was terrified of them skiing, which is a big deal in Canada. Some of my patients ignored what I said and went and did it anyway, so far without any disasters. I now tell patients that if they skied at instructor level, which is surprisingly common in Canada, they can go back to it, but if at green level, they should not. And I tell them they should not ski at weekends when some five-year-old child coming down the hill at fifty kilometers will run across their ski tips.

One of the problems was that these implants were expensive. This meant that only a few countries could afford it. One thing we looked at was to try to make implants cheaper. There are problems with that, of course. If implants are too cheap, then there is no money to develop better implants. We see that today. Some countries that should be at the leading edge only allow into their country old design implants that are obsolete elsewhere. When that was only the third world, it did not matter, but it matters today. Fortunately, there are some farsighted countries, such as South Korea, that are investing in the future.

I wanted to make a cheap and cheerful hip joint, as most surgeons can put one in, sort of, at any rate better than nothing. We were looking at materials, and the cheapest we could find was stainless steel. I really did not want to use that for a variety of reasons, one being that it has nickel in it, and patients who have a metal allergy are usually allergic to nickel, but if there was nothing else, I would. I was operating one day when I got a panic phone call from the company in Memphis I was working with. Someone had dumped ten tons of titanium on the market that morning at an unbelievable price. The nurses held the phone to my ear as I listened.

"What to do?"

I had no hesitation and asked them to buy it all. Titanium is a very light metal. With that amount of titanium, I could replace the hip of everyone in the world. The only people using that amount of titanium were the Russians, who used it to build their nuclear submarines. So I knew someone in Russia had stolen it, and we had to get it before someone stole it back. I heard they dumped a large block of it in the front yard of the engineer in Memphis whom I was working with on the project.

I used that cemented hip for about fifteen years in elderly patients, as we were very short of funds in the Canadian health-care system, and it worked very well, but the profit margin was not enough for the company to continue its use. Cheap and cheerful is not something Americans are interested in, and America drives the rest of the world.

I was still looking for something to use in young people that could be disassembled when it wore out. I was looking for something like car brakes. When the brakes wear out, one changes the brakes, not the whole car. Eventually, I found it. It was a design from a Russian called Sivash. It did not work at all, not a tiny bit, but all I need is the idea, and I can make it work. There I go again, saying I! It is never I, and I have known that since I studied bioengineering in Glasgow.

My old friend Tim McTighe had joined that company, and with some very clever engineers, like Fred DiCarlo and Doug Noiles, we came up with a design that was so radically different that when we showed it to Bill Murray, the professor in San Francisco, he asked if we were really serious about putting that in a human being. Again, this was in the days before the government decided that they knew everything and that they were going to help. The first government man appointed to help regulate orthopedics in Canada was a nuclear power plant supervisor. Quite what nuclear power plants have to do with orthopedic surgery is a mystery, which only a government man would understand.

If I sound bitter, it is because I am. I was the chairman of that section in Canada, and we had just passed a motion, and I knew that because I proposed it—that government oversight was unnecessary. If they were bound and determined to have government control, then simply insist that implants pass the European Union ISO 9000 or the American 510(k). Instead, they insisted that bureaucrats with no medical or engineering experience have oversight and that every bit of stuff coming in to Canada be inspected by these experts. Oh well, I guess everyone's idiot son needs a job.

Anyway, it took about two years to finalize the design of the new hip. The reason it took so long was that variations had to be tried out in humans, as there were no animal models. For example, there were all sorts of finishes one could put on a product. Too rough and the bone would stick to it, which is advantageous in some areas, but not in others. Too smooth and the cost went up unnecessarily, and people were paying for it. The lower the fixation point, the better the bone ingrowth, but the more stress shielding it was above the lowest fixation point. None of this is major, but it all has to be answered. The eventual design was so good that it had not changed in almost thirty years, and the usual life cycle of an implant was about seven years.

The only change we made was for the tiny elderly people in Japan, and that was simply a size issue. But as size alters the properties of materials and as manufacturing tolerances become more difficult to control at a smaller size, it did prove interesting, although it was fun to work on. As the physical size of each generation in Japan seems to be increasing dramatically, that version of the hip will become an interesting historical side note, similar to the tiny shoes worn by Chinese women in the foot-binding era.

CHAPTER 25

THE ROAD WARRIORS

I do not want to pretend that the history I was told of about some of these road warriors is entirely accurate. At my editor's insistence, I have changed some of the names and left out the worst stories. Most of them I heard about in dim bars late at night in strange cities, which is where one used to hear the important things first. I called them "whispers in the wind." I heard a whisper in the wind in a bar in Korea from Dr. Park once. He said that he thought there was a problem with metal on metal bearings, but he did not know why. As I had heard a similar thing from Hans Willert in Germany a few months before, I immediately stopped using them. I have always believed that if clever men think there is a problem, stop until they can work out what the problem is.

I had been part of a study group for the FDA on metal/metal bearings. If they worked, they would not likely ever wear out in the lifetime of a human. I did about 150 cases and never had problems with the bearing, and fifteen years later, I still do not, so I was not sure where the problems Dr. Park was seeing were coming from. Several years later, we think we know. It never was the bearing. It was because it was technically possible with a thin metal cup to put a much larger head on the implant. The advantage of this is that it will reduce the dislocation rate, making the surgery technically easier to do. I never used anything larger than a thirty-two-millimeter head, and it was mostly twenty-eight millimeters, which I used exclusively for the metal/metal study. When heads of thirty-six millimeters and up were used, it led to extra strain on the junction of the head and the stem, and that was the problem. In other words, engineering 101. Basic principles cannot be ignored.

It is like the Kipling poem "Gods of the Copybook Headings:"

> We were living in trees when they met us. They showed us each in turn
> That water would certainly wet us, and fire would certainly burn
> But we found them lacking in uplift, vision and breadth of mind
> So we left them to teach the gorillas, while we followed the march of mankind.
> And it goes on, that presently word would come, that a tribe had been wiped off its ice field or the lights had gone out in Rome.
> As it will be in the future, it was in the birth of man,
> There are only three things certain since social progress began.
> That the dog returns to his vomit, and the sow returns to her mire,
> And the burnt fool's bandaged fingers go wobbling back to the fire.

The problem is that when burned, instead of managing the fire, the tendency is to put it out. Once it was realized that junctions could be a problem, the temptation was to get rid of the junctions. I used the first taper-lock junctions in North America, given to me by a friend of mine, a famous surgeon from the Saar in Germany. I used them for two years before they were released in North America, so that is forty years of experience.

There is a story told about him. Some US surgeons were watching him operate. He used very few guides, as he had done a huge volume of surgeries. One of the visitors asked him about guides. The surgeon is reported to have stopped operating and turned and looked at the questioner and said, "Are you a surgeon or a gynecologist?"

It was definitely not the way to gain adherents to your cause. I was once visiting him, and he took me to his home, which was built on the side of a hill. He had a tunnel, which ran back into the hill, with a survival chamber with food and water. He told me, "You [expletives] bombed me in Munich when I was a boy. Try to bomb me now."

Remember, these were in the days when the Russians were not far away, and war was predicted every summer. One spring, I forgot why, I was convinced that the Russians would be coming across the Fulda Gap when the soil dried out, so I bought a large amount of dried food and containers for water. I knew if I could stay indoors for the first few days after the nuclear bombs exploded, I would avoid the worst of the radiation. Then the Vatican elected a Polish cardinal as pope, and I knew the Cold War was over, as there was no way the Red Army would get through. The railway lines necessary to transport tanks to Germany ran through Poland, and if the pope asked the Poles to cut the lines, they would. I ate dried food for the next year.

I was also working on a double-tapered hip that had all sorts of advantages. In the first version, we made a mistake, and one of the tapers was too short and too thin. The first one broke when a patient of Dickie Jones was wrestling a steer during a rodeo competition. I had two breaks as well, so we pulled it off the market immediately, doubled the strength of the taper, and significantly lengthened it. Since it was reintroduced twelve years ago, there had been no problems, but tapers now have bad reputation for other reasons that are too complex and inflammatory to go into here.

There were about five major joint replacement companies in the world, mostly American. Each had three or four surgeon champions or road warriors. These surgeons crisscrossed the world teaching the techniques of joint replacement, especially the joint they were championing. There were about twenty of us, mainly Americans. We used to meet in odd places, such as the superb business class lounge in Narita airport in Tokyo. It was not very luxurious, but it had so many computer jacks that all working men tried to get there because there were so few jacks in other lounges. Computer batteries in those days did not last long, and we always had to be preparing for the next talk. I always flew with a spare battery.

Bill was one of the early road warriors. The town he grew up in was largely Italian immigrants and was so small that it was called Wellhead Number Nine, in Pennsylvania, I think. Bill was the first person from there ever to go to university. He did it on a football scholarship to Rutgers. Bill was not a big man, but he was solid. God help the blocker who stood between Bill and a university scholarship. That would have been a world of hurt. High school football in the US can be brutal. I first met Bill when I was a fellow in London. He was traveling around Europe, as we all did, trying to sort out who and what was believable.

It never ceased to amaze me how much junk science was out there and how many people believed it. Clearly, statistics was a lost art and even common sense.

Bill was one of the few nervous speakers I knew. Most of us were showmen anyway or, at least, learned to give that impression. Nonetheless, he stuck with it grimly for quite a few years, mostly inside the US. There were not actually that many who liked it outside the US. In the early days, the insertion of some hips was a little difficult. If the implant was too small, it would come loose, and if too large, the femur (thighbone) would split and have to be wired like a barrel hoop. Bill used to call these telltale wires the "badge of courage."

Fritz used to wrestle All-American when he was in school. He was a big man. It must have been terrible for these neat, compact little wrestlers to meet Fritz.

He and an engineer developed a new concept of mobile bearing, which was quite revolutionary in reducing plastic wear when that was a serious problem. I especially liked to hang around New Orleans with Fritz, because while that is a really fun town, it is pretty dangerous, but he was not someone to be trifled with. He developed a very good ankle replacement, and I used it for many years.

He and I did some different things. One problem for which initially we had no solution was what to do when the kneecap was missing. We did develop some different operations, one being an auto graft bone patella, but the numbers were never enough to enable us to refine them. Fortunately, surgeons stopped taking out kneecaps, so that problem went away. He once sent me a case of body dysmorphism from the US. The patient wanted her ankles thinned. I saw her between OR cases and was thinking that I actually could do it. I told the girls in the operating room. They quickly brought me to my senses, suggesting I was as mentally disturbed as the patient.

Leo was another famous road warrior, with his Harley-Davidson and his pit bulls. He came from hardscrabble Texas and funded his way through school by boxing, mainly in Mexico, because he was underage. He told me the only thing he ever learned about fighting was not to do it. He said the Mexicans were so macho they refused to fall down, and he would get arm weary hitting them. He started off running a very well-attended course in St. Louis. I remember going to talk there once.

I had just been married, and my wife was with me. We were on a late-night Friday flight from Chicago. The business class was full of businessmen going home for the weekend, so the alcohol was flowing freely. My wife and I were drinking champagne. Just before we landed, the stewardess came to pick up the bottle, which still had some left. The man behind leaned over and told the stewardess we were just married and to leave the bottle with us. It was a pretty friendly flight, as it used to be on Friday evenings. When we got off the plane, the stewardess gave us a freshly opened bottle of champagne and two glasses, so we celebrated in the limo going downtown. That was when flying was fun. It no longer is.

Leo used to run a course in San Diego at the Coronado Hotel, which used to be the largest wooden structure in the US. What was fascinating about that place was watching the Navy SEALs and some other special forces training on the beach, which went on forever and was cordoned off for the military only. These men seemed to be able to swim across the San Diego Bay. He was once visiting me in Toronto. I took him home with me. Some French surgeons had been visiting me the week before and had given me a bottle of brandy, which had a very fancy wax seal. I opened it and gave Leo a glass. Leo, who actually does not drink much, opened his eyes wide and asked for more. It really was the absolute best brandy I ever tasted.

I once ran into Leo at breakfast in the business class floor in the Shilla Hotel in Seoul. He had been out with Korean surgeons the night before and was not very chipper. I have a suspicion that Koreans and Finns are related somehow, as they are very different from other Orientals. I know their grammar is different, and they can certainly drink differently. In Japan, after a few drinks, people tend to fall down. Half the Chinese cannot drink at all because they lack the enzyme to metabolize alcohol, but the Koreans have hollow legs and can drink like Finns. I used to be able to drink a fair amount, but in Korea, I would never drink anything with color, like scotch, as I knew it would not be good the next day. I preferred to drink Korean soju, which is colorless, and the lack of congeners results in much less hangover.

Dickie Jones was another character. He was the quintessential Texan, but like my Parisian friend Philippe Cartier, I don't think he actually came from Texas originally. He wore Hawaiian shirts and running shoes everywhere. Before the rise of computer-based knowledge, he ran huge

---

pre-exam courses in Dallas for young orthopedic surgeons, so he was very well-known. He was very clever and developed some of the braces, which are still commonly used in the US, before selling his very profitable brace-making company. There was the famous story told about him rafting down the Grand Canyon, mooning the tourists on the rim.

I met him when he came to visit me in Toronto to see what funny things I was doing. He scrubbed with me when I was revising a hip joint. I changed the socket and tested the stem. It seemed reasonably tight, so I told Dickie that I was going to leave it. Dickie, who had come up from Dallas to see this, gripped the stem and pulled it straight out of the patient's femur.

"There," he said, "now you have to revise it."

He was right, and I was wrong. If he could pull it out, then it was loose enough that it should have been revised. If it had not been changed then, the patient would have needed further surgery in a year or two. I told the patient who had a very bad rheumatoid, whom I had known for about twenty years and who was a very, very courageous lady, about this episode; and she sent Dickie a thank-you note.

Then there was Tom Mallory. Just the other day, I got word Tom had passed on. His wife once gave him a Christmas present. What do you give the man who has everything? She gave him a mink mat for his Rolls-Royce. Everything Tom touched turned to gold. He was a fellow in some unit when the first licenses for the use of bone cement were given out in the US. The man he was working for did not particularly want it, so Tom asked for it and was given it. It was a license to print money.

Tom promptly moved to Columbus, Ohio, and began putting in hips. For years, his only competition in the Midwest was Merrill Ritter, another fabulous surgeon. They used to compete to see who was the fastest hip in the West. He was breathtakingly prescient. When the downtown post office came up for sale, Tom bought it and used it for his main office and a physiotherapy unit. It was prime real estate downtown, before people wanted to live downtown. He bought a gentlemen's entertainment club when it came up for sale. The parking was great, and the large number of small rooms was ideal for doctors' offices. He and Bill Head developed one of the best-selling hips in the world, and twenty-five years later, it still sells very well. Once, I looked at being a professor in Ohio State University. One of my stipulations was that I would take the job if Tom Mallory could be my ramrod. He was so successful that the university people hated him so much that that was a complete anathema.

That happened one other time. The professor's job came up in Tucson, Arizona. I had no intention of applying for it, but a friend of mine, Colonel Brucknell, encouraged me to apply. He was retiring from the US military and wanted to live there. He said if I became the professor, he would be my ramrod. He explained that he would be able to lift all burdens from my shoulders because having been a military doctor all his life, he had "bullshit" on which the military and universities run, down to a fine art.

He was hilarious. I was in San Antonio once, and I heard him lecturing to some of the military surgeons in language they would understand.

"Scout your position. Consolidate your resources. Make a battle plan and a fallback plan. Remember what Clausewitz said, that no plan survives contact with the enemy."

He once attended a course I was chairing in Edinburgh. He took some time off and drove around Scotland, staying in bed-and-breakfast places. He said he had a wonderful time, as the man in almost every house was a veteran. So they would sit all night, drink scotch, and talk about old battles.

Chit Ranawat used to take his whole operating team from New York to India once a year. He would do about thirty knee replacements. He showed the Indian populace that knee replacement could be trusted when on one trip he did both knees of the sitting prime minister. When Chit went, he booked the whole front end of a 747.

It was not only surgeons, there were also engineers who were on the road, like Seth Greenwald; Ian Clarke, whom I had known in Strathclyde in Glasgow when I was studying engineering; Harry Mckillop; Phil Noble; and John Fisher from Leeds in England. I would often learn from them what they were thinking long before it was published. The last time I met John Fisher was when I noticed him at breakfast in the Shilla Hotel in Seoul. Come to think of it, the last time I met Ian Clarke and Harry McKillop was also on different trips to Korea, so maybe the Koreans want to meet engineers rather than surgeons.

CHAPTER 26

WE BAND OF BROTHERS

At its peak, I was in Europe or the Far East about once a month for more than twenty years. All that was required were zopiclone, a long-acting sleeping pill for flights over eight hours in length, and halcion for short flights of about six or seven hours to get to Europe, as these medications left no hangover. One did sometimes have a little difficulty with short-term memory with halcion. Once, I was going to Brussels. I know I got off the plane in Charles De Gaulle in Paris, crossed the airport, and got on a flight to Brussels; but I don't remember doing so. Not that it matters, as I have been in Charles De Gaulle often enough. The other thing that one needed was melatonin. One needs that for the first couple of days after arrival in a different time zone.

Usually on the third day, one stops the sleeping pills and the melatonin. That night is interesting because one catches up on REM sleep, which the sleeping pills suppress. I don't know if it happened to others, but I always got nightmares the whole of that night. What was interesting was that the worst nightmare was always the same. I was standing on an empty, flat, grassless plain. The light was funny, and there was a palpable sense of menace that something really bad was going to appear, but it never did. It was only on the nightmare night I ever got that one. Once nightmare night was over, time zone adaption was complete, until of course one returned home, when the whole process would repeat.

Nightmares, or dreams, are funny, and no one quite understands them. I first became a parent in middle age, and after the birth of my first child, I got a nightmare regularly. It was always the same. The child had fallen into the water and was sinking. I was swimming down after him, but he was sinking faster than I could swim. He would get deeper and deeper, and then I would wake up. After the birth of my second child, that nightmare went away and never came back.

The other way to counteract jet lag is exercise. I found that I would waken up at 5:00 a.m. in any case, so I could spend an hour or so in the gym before going to work. Usually, work was over by 5:00 p.m., so another hour or so in the gym was feasible before going out in the evening.

We traveling men used to joke that the best place in the world was thirty thousand feet up in the air. There, the responsibility rested with the man driving the plane. We had no responsibility for anything, and the next few hours were ours and ours alone. Even that was not entirely true, because every lecture was different, and we were prepared on the plane wherever we were going.

But the sense of relief was palpable when the limo would pull up outside the hospital, and I would leave the operating room or office and was on the way to the airport. For years, I refused to carry a cell phone. I got one once, but people kept calling me, so I got rid of it. If someone needed to speak to me, they could speak to my secretary, and she would decide if I needed to speak to them. The anonymity of the VIP lounge at an airport was wonderful. One could sit and sort out the lecture or make up new ones or analyze research data without anyone showing the slightest interest. It was the same on the plane—the blissful, quiet anonymity. Have a few drinks, do some work, read a little, pop a pill, and go to sleep, knowing that someone would pick you up at the airport.

Actually, someone did not pick me up at the airport on a couple of occasions. I arrived in Reno, Nevada, late one night, and there was no one there. I knew the meeting was in a hotel in Tahoe, but I did not know which one. I started calling the Tahoe casinos because it would have to be one of them. I had been careless and did not have any information with me, so I did not even know the name of the conference. I asked the hotel switchboards if they had a booking for me. The first half dozen did not. Sometimes the booking would not be in my name, so I stopped and went to a hotel in Reno for the night. I should have kept calling because the next hotel in the phone book was the right one.

In the morning, I phoned the head office, got the address, and drove to Tahoe. It actually worked out quite well because the drive up along the lake was quite spectacular, and if I had gone at night, I would never have seen it.

That happened to me once in Tokyo as well. I phoned my Japanese minder, Humi Hirai, and begged her to come and rescue me.

"Now, now," she said, or the Japanese equivalent, "Man up. It will be all right," and gave me detailed instructions on how to take the train downtown.

Once, when I had not been in the game long and felt that I was a crucial player, there was a ski meeting on Snowmass, I think. I was on the last plane leaving Denver, and the engine blew up at the end of the runway, so I was stuck. I was supposed to give the first talk in the morning, so I rented a car and drove overnight. I thought the car was a gutless wonder because it would not go very fast, especially climbing the mountains. It was just as well because in the morning, I found the white stuff on the roads on which I had been driving was ice.

Kenny was a dandy. I once spent an evening with him trying to explain to me how to iron a pocket square so that it came to four points, or was it three? Mosby Year Book asked me to write a book telling surgeons how to do hip replacement. I asked them how I was supposed to do that. They said, "Just copy Kenny's book on knee replacement. Where he says knee, just put in hip."

He was a great knee replacement surgeon. I was going out to operate in a place I knew Kenny had recently been, so I asked him what it was like. The first thing he said was "Bring your own saw." Some Europeans used a saw blade that was very flexible. That was fine if you were cutting through things, but not so fine if you were cutting off things and wanted a flat surface. Some of these blades were so flexible you could flick peanuts with them. I had had problems with that before, but I knew a girl in the US who could make saw blades, and she made very stiff ones for me.

If I had been smart, I would have bankrolled her, because she became one of the biggest saw blade makers in the world. The blade I use myself is very stiff, but even so, I had a fellow once, Roger, who was a big strong rugby player. When he cut knees for me, the surface was wavy, like sand dunes. I was asking him, "Roger, what the [expletive] are you doing?"

when I realized he was pushing the blade. He was so strong he could bend even a stiff blade.

Speaking of saw blades, I once took that problem to my engineering class in Waterloo University. One of the boys did a thesis on how to make a saw blade that would not whip or bend. His design ended up being two reciprocating blades, just like an electric carving knife.

So I took Kenny's advice about this country and took my own saw. These were battery-powered and looked like an Uzi. Just try getting something like that on cabin baggage nowadays.

The other thing Kenny told me was that when he was there, they had just had a case of gas gangrene in their main operating room, so he did a demonstration knee replacement in the emergency department.

I was operating there, and it was being videoed out to the audience in the auditorium. The cables from the huge camera they were using were trailing on the scrub nurse's sterile table. I was horrified, but no one else seemed to be concerned, so I casually asked them what their infection rate was. They said it was not a problem; it was under 20 percent.

Wayne was another road warrior. He was a true Russian, he said, and over the centuries, the Russian stomach had become adapted to eat potatoes, cabbage, beetroot, and a little pork, nothing else. He had been operating in France for a week, and they kept giving him this awful slop, like foie gras and snails and frog legs, for God's sake, which he could not possibly eat. He thought he was going to die of hunger; when they were driving him into Paris and he saw the golden arches of McDonald's, he knew his life was saved.

We all had some interesting experiences. I was once operating in a place where they usually do not turn on the air-conditioning until May, and this was April. There was a heat wave, and I was dripping sweat into the wound. So they turned it on. The ducts had not been cleaned yet, so the whole room turned black, including the incision. The surgeon told me later that the wound healed without incident, and the patient was fine.

Most times, one never finds out the result of this itinerant surgery unless it turned out to be a disaster. One lady I did in Lillehammer in Norway did send me a postcard every anniversary of her surgery for about fifteen years.

Traveling inside the US was easy then, as there were no terrorists and therefore no or minimal security. After the Twin Towers, it turned crazy, where in the name of equity, they were searching nuns and women with little children. Instead of getting to the airport at the last moment, it was now necessary to arrive a couple of hours ahead of flight time. Most meetings in the US used to be teaching rounds, which were always held on Friday mornings at 7:00 a.m., so it was necessary to get there the night before. If anyone really needed help with surgery, that could be arranged also. One small company I worked for hired two operating room nurses who covered the US: one for the eastern half and the other for the western side. They would scrub for cases if the surgeon had not done the operation before and talk him through it. These girls were in two or three different towns a week for a year or more, before they burned out and went back to their own operating rooms and were replaced with fresh nurses. They were incredible women. No one ever disrespected them because they worked for Tom Mallory from Columbus or John Brothers from Nashville, and no one in the US would cross these men.

There were all sorts of meetings. Hans Willert once held a meeting in Göttingen in December. Germany at Christmas is very beautiful. I was once at a meeting in Munich at that time, so I took the opportunity to see some of Bavaria. Neuschwanstein, Mad King Ludwig's castle, is one of the wonders of the world. Everyone has seen photographs of it. Sadly, I cannot remember if it was a sleigh or a carriage that took us up the hill, but whatever it was, it was horse-drawn. That night, I do remember we were in a hotel on the edge of a frozen lake in Fusen. Great magical bands of mist came rolling in across the ice.

Göttingen on that December night was a picture postcard, which it is not by day. It was all lights and music and stalls in the marketplace and glistening snow and ice and some of their specialty gingerbread. Hans finished the meeting with a competition on plastic bones for which he gave prizes. I got the prize for the fastest modular hip insertion. Since the certificate is in German, which almost none of my patients can read, I had it framed, and it hangs on the wall of my office as a badge of honor. I do remember he gave Peter Griss, a senior German surgeon, the prize for the best-dressed orthopedic surgeon.

The biggest meeting of joint replacement surgeons in the world is called the Current Concepts. It is now held in Orlando every December. I used to take the last flight out of Toronto, as I was usually operating. For years, it would always snow that evening, which led to hours of nail-biting in case Air Canada chicken out and refuse to fly.

I was once operating in St. John's in Newfoundland when it began to snow, really snow. I had done two knee replacements and was beginning the third. By the time I had finished that, it looked pretty grim, so we canceled the last case, and the surgeon who had invited me took me in his four-by-four out to the airport. The road was unrecognizable as the snow was so deep, and I had a distinct impression we were driving over people's backyards. When we got to the airport, I found that Air Canada had chickened out, but another airline was going to try to make it. That airline was a small one, whose initials were EPA, which I was told stood for Every Passenger Anxious. These were great guys; they took off in a blinding snowstorm and got me back to Toronto to operate the next day. Cowboys they may have been, but I did admire them.

The Canadian winter can make things quite interesting. I was once somewhere in the US when it began to really snow in Toronto, so they canceled the inbound flights. I had a very big operating list booked for the next day, so I was desperate to get back. I was with one of the Canadian salesmen. We managed to get a flight to Detroit and rented a car there. Larry drove from there to Toronto by night, through a raging blizzard. It was quite hair-raising, but I managed to sleep a little. Larry somehow avoided sliding off the road or being hit by a sliding truck and got me to the hospital just in time to get some coffee and start operating.

The first couple of Current Concepts meetings were in Miami Beach about thirty years ago. I was a speaker at the second meeting and have been ever since, until a year or so ago. At that meeting, there were more faculty than attendees, but now there are over two thousand orthopedic surgeons who would come. Like many American meetings, the timing is rigid. You are told how many minutes you have to speak, no more, no less. Non-Americans tend to run into problems with that. In Europe, it tends to be the bigger the professor, the longer the speech. If you do that once at this meeting, you are not coming back. It is run by Seth Greenwald, an engineer from the Projects in New York. Europeans do not know what the Projects are. Suffice it to say that those who get out are pretty exceptional. Seth did his PhD at Oxford and is the best-known bioengineer in the US.

This meeting is largely a series of debates. Seth says you do not have to believe something; you just have to argue it. Everyone knows that truth is likely somewhere in the middle, but Seth asks the speakers to take the extreme position. The talks are recorded on videos and disks or memory sticks and are sent to every orthopedic school in the world, or at least the known world. For the last ten years, a second meeting has been held in Las Vegas in May, which now attracts large numbers of surgeons from the Far East.

The largest meetings used to be the national meetings, but these tried to span the whole of the field of orthopedics. As the fields are now so subspecialized, these meetings are now becoming less relevant and are being replaced by more specialized meetings such as Current Concepts.

CHAPTER 27

THE OPERATING ROOM

The operating room is where life is real for a surgeon, or it used to be. Times are changing. The training to be a surgeon used to be fairly intense. I was on call every second night for almost five years, and yet I remember Robert Judet in Paris laughing at how little surgery I had done. No one complained about the training. If you complained, you were out, which we felt was as it should be. An operating room is not a place for snowflakes. If you fray around the edges, do not come here. If you can't stand the heat, get out of the kitchen. It is not a place where there is an "every surgeon gets a trophy" day. Touchy-feely it is not. But maybe things are changing.

About thirty years ago, I was examining medical students. I was with a belly surgeon. He would ask the orthopedic questions, and I would ask the general surgery questions. We thought that since I had only done six months of general surgery and he had done no orthopedics, our knowledge might be what a medical student might be expected to know. One student killed three theoretical patients in a row, so we failed him. The solid waste hit the fan. How dare we fail a U of T medical student! The fact that he was stupid and utterly incompetent did not seem to matter. I stopped examining medical students for twenty years, as I was uninterested in playing charades. I returned to it ten years ago. Now there are virtually no words spoken during an examination; it is simply a tick-off sheet of paper, so I do it to fulfill my statutory duty.

Training to be a surgeon is an apprenticeship like a plumber or a carpenter. It is like sports. When I was training with my brother's coaching group doing reps of two-hundred-meter sprints, you vomited, then you did some more. If you do not want to do it, do not do it. Marshal Zhukov used to say of the Red Army, "Train hard, fight easy." I always thought that in the OR, the case should be routine, no thought required, and in orthopedic surgery, there should be very little excitement. I had one case where a patient had a cardiac arrest during a hip replacement. The nurses were superb. They had him flipped over onto his back, got him going again, and we finished the operation. Other than that, I do not remember any earthshaking excitement.

An operating room tends to be a noisy place as we use a lot of power tools. Once, a company produced a new saw that was so noisy I thought it was inexcusable. I contacted the ministry of health and got a machine to measure noise, which I wore all day. I was hoping to show the company that what they had produced was illegal, and so hopefully, they would have to hire me as a consultant, because I was sure I could put in sound baffles. Unfortunately, while the sound was far above the legal limit, the duration of the illegal noise did not go on for long enough. I should have had one of my slower colleagues wear the device.

I moved to the orthopedic hospital part-time in 1978, because Jim Bateman took me around to meet the rheumatologists who worked there and suggested they feed me arthritic patients, which they did. That was so magnanimous of Big Jim, because he was also a joint replacement surgeon, having developed the bipolar hip, which is used by all the trauma surgeons in the world to this day, something which people seem to have forgotten. The orthopedic hospital was a joint replacement surgeon's dream. It was eighty beds only, purely orthopedics, and so small that everyone knew everyone else.

After my first divorce, Ms. Ellen, who was the head cleaner in the operating room, looked after me. She was Jamaican, and she knew that Scottish men are like Jamaican men; they have no idea how to cook. So for almost a year, every weekend, I got the children. She used to make a large goat curry casserole, and there is nothing better than Ms. Ellen's Jamaican goat curry.

For a while, I worked in both hospitals. But one day, in 1982, I added up the number of patients I had in the hospital, and it came to over forty. That was way too many, so I resigned from the Toronto General. This was a frightening thing to do, as it meant I no longer would be doing trauma, which is the bread and butter and mortgage payments of all young orthopedic surgeons.

This was quite different from the teaching hospital. Ms. O'Connor was the nurse in charge, and she was really in charge. Her head nurses were like the sisters I had known in Scotland. They had no university nursing degrees, but they knew every patient on their floor. If an operating list got booked, it got finished, no matter what time it took. There were really only three young surgeons there. One of them was my partner Peter Welsh, who was from New Zealand. He had been an athlete, winning gold in the Commonwealth steeplechase. His main interest was shoulders. Once, he was speaking in Japan and told them that he had done over four hundred repairs for dislocating shoulders. The Japanese, whose numbers in comparison were tiny, did not believe him.

Times have changed, and standard behavior then would not be acceptable now. Romances were common, and no one cared. In the Toronto General Hospital, there was a TGIF (thank God it's Friday) party every Friday in the hospital, where the wine and beer flowed freely from 5:00 p.m. to 7:30 p.m. At the orthopedic hospital, the surgeons kept the operating room fridge full of white wine. If the case ran late, as it sometimes did until 8:00 p.m., at its close, everyone would have a glass of wine. The married girls would go home, mostly, and the rest would go for dinner for which the surgeon paid and then go and party.

Our favorite was a tiny restaurant just beside the hospital. It was a Spanish restaurant called Segovia, and the chef was from Segovia. When things got quiet, he would play his Spanish guitar. Once, I had a patient from Nova Scotia send me a case of live lobsters, simply wrapped in wet newspaper in a cardboard carton. I took that to the restaurant, and the chef served lobster to my operating room team and all his regular patrons that night.

My partner Peter Welsh had an indoor swimming pool and hot tub, so on particularly raucous nights following a late operating room, everyone— nurses, orderlies, physiotherapists, and doctors—would go there. Clothes were optional. Things slowly changed over the next decade or so. No one said no; it just became no. Perhaps we simply got older, and the freedom symbolized by Woodstock went away. I remember I was trying to educate one particularly obtuse resident. In exasperation, I told him that breasts face the front, a statement of the obvious. My scrub nurse said, "Not always, sir, mine face the floor." I don't think anyone would say that in an operating room now.

Just remembering her makes me feel bad. I always felt that personal problems should be left outside the operating room, but that nurse's husband or boyfriend abandoned her, and she was really broken up to the extent that it showed in her work. Looking back in sorrow, I think, What would it have cost me to have been a little nicer?

When I moved across full-time from the Toronto General, I took some staff with me from the operating room. Some of the people who had been there initially moved on to other places. We stayed in touch for years. It was eventually called the Dinosaur Club, made up of the OR staff from Toronto General from the '70s. We manage to meet for dinner once a year, but the numbers decrease year after year. One of the ladies at dinner with me this year was ninety-seven years old.

Since a lot of the scrub nurses were from the Caribbean Islands, we had a loose organization, which we called the Jamaican Mafia. My wife was ill and needed surgery in the middle of the SARS epidemic in Toronto. Toronto went crazy over that, a good example of total mismanagement. In Toronto, they first moved infected patients from one hospital to another, thus contaminating them all. Having done that, they closed the hospitals for weeks. I was in Chicago lecturing then. Because my hospital, which never had a single case, was closed by government edict, I asked them what they were doing. The answer was nothing. The sick patients were in the hospital that that was why there were hospitals. I was having difficulty getting my wife's surgery, so the organization swung into action. One of the girls who had been in Toronto General with me, Sheila, had moved to be head nurse of the operating room in that hospital. She had retired, but she phoned the operating room every half hour until my wife got done. Unfair, favoritism, you bet. We tried to look after our own.

One of my favorite nurses, Octavia, who was a really serious woman, won the lottery and went back to St. Vincent in the Caribbean. Octavia scrubbed everything, which was on her table, including the kitchen sink.

Bev Scott, who was from Jamaica, came with me and stayed with me until she retired. She was always so gracious. Everyone goes through what is called the young surgeon syndrome, where they get hot and bothered and shouted a lot. Bev's handling was always impeccable. When the case was finished, she would take me aside and say, "I need to talk to you.

That was unkind and unhelpful and uncalled for, and I want an apology immediately."

She always got her apology immediately. She was so good that a couple of Swedish surgeons who were visiting me offered her the head job in their hospital. They were nice men, so Bev considered it until she checked a map to see where they came from. It was Umeo, which is about as far north as you can get before the ice begins. I was there once, and the only entertainment was when the ferry came in from somewhere, perhaps Estonia, and everyone got drunk on duty-free alcohol.

Bev scrubbed for me for about fifteen years, then she said no more. Joint replacement surgery is physically heavy surgery not only for the surgeon but also for the nurses. The Americans brought in something called the OSHA rules, which mandated that the OR trays could not weigh more than twenty pounds. This gave us designers real headaches, as it was difficult to keep the weight of the instruments under that, and we often spent as much time on the tray design as on the instruments.

Instruments are heavy because they are subjected to such physical abuse. If they are made delicate, they break. We tried plastic trays to reduce the weight, but they broke so often they had to be withdrawn. I always tried to keep it to a minimum, but the demand for instruments was there, especially by surgeons who did not do the operation often. One company had five twenty-pound trays of instruments for a knee replacement.

Bev moved to arthroscopy, which was much lighter, and stayed there until she retired. Even after retirement, she kept working, supervising home care nurses. When my wife was ill, Bev was visiting her socially. A nurse came in to change the dressings. Bev, who never suffered fools gladly, was deeply unimpressed.

"Where are your gloves, girl?"

"I don't have any."

"Well, you just wait. I have gloves in my car, and do not come into this house again without gloves."

Another person I took with me was Finbar, who was from the island of Grenada. He was a superb operating room orderly. That meant he brought the patients into the operating room, helped position them, held the limb while we were preparing the skin, and did myriad of other things that make an OR function. He was gay, which bothered no one. He was so kind to the patients that they all loved him. I remember when my father was dying. A man of that era was embarrassed about his loss of control of his bodily functions.

"Till the body triumphed and the last poor shame departed."

My father was always grateful when it was male orderlies who came to clean him. Finbar sadly ultimately went off to work in New York in the middle of the AIDS epidemic and died there.

The other one who came with me was Edna Quammie, who came to Canada from Connecticut. She once showed me photographs of herself in her one-room schoolhouse. I thought I knew something about her she did not know herself. She was spelling her name wrong. It should not have been Quammie. The proper spelling, I thought, should be Kwame. I took to mean that she had been a princess in Africa, and I treated her as one all my life. After I had written this, I fact-checked it and wished I had not. Kwame sounded like kaiser or czar to me. In Twi, it actually means "born on Saturday." That should be a lesson—do not fact-check your dreams.

When I first went to Toronto General as a junior resident, I met Ms. Quammie. I used to sit in the nursing station with her in the evening. I would order beer for the patients, and she and I would drink it, feet up in the desk. I was still the strong boy then, and she was the slim girl, so when we did evening rounds on the patients, I would carry her in my arms. That was 1972, and no patient ever objected. She would come and go, a new interest or a new job or something, but she always came back, and we still have lunch together occasionally after almost fifty years since we first met.

When my wife was really sick, I was sitting at her bedside in the hospital. The curtains pulled back, and a voice said, "Go home now. I will look after her."

One of the greatest nurses in the world had arrived, and all would be well.

CHAPTER 28

THE NEXT GENERATION

When Bev and Edna got tired, I wondered who would take over. I came into the OR one day, and a tall woman I had never met was shouting at one of our more hapless nurses, "I come here to work. You came here to work. If you do not want to work, go home!"

I went onto the operating room and embraced her.

"Tall woman, I think I am in love!"

It was Mira. She was originally from Serbia and had one of these long, lean Serbian faces with high cheekbones and heavy eyebrows. She was strikingly beautiful. For years, she had worked running operating rooms in Libya and had loved it, but with two teenage daughters, it was time to move on, so she came to Canada. She was so clever and worked so hard. One of my great sorrows was that I made her tear up once. I felt so stricken and so guilty. How could I ever have done anything so stupid?

I thought that I had been cured of the young surgeon syndrome years ago. I was hooting and hollering in the operating room about something, I forget what. The scrub nurse who was a big Irish girl said, "I don't have to take this shit!"

I stopped immediately. She was absolutely correct. She did not have to take this shit, and I tried never to do it again.

The second of the triumvirate was Roland. He was a full-blooded Delaware Indian. He was a big man. He never got tired and never seemed to need a break. He would, if allowed, scrub for every single case. He was so confident in his own ability that he would ask the anesthetist to bring the patient into the OR while he was washing his hands to set up. Most nurses need about twenty minutes minimum to set up before they will allow the patient into the room, and I have certainly seen as long as forty minutes.

Roland was gay, which was why he spent so much of his time in Toronto, as opposed to the Indian reservation. His family had accumulated land outside the reservation over the generations, so he had a large farm, where he grew sweet corn and melons. He thought the only good farmworkers were the Mennonite girls with their long skirts and their century-old bonnets, so he hired them to pick his corn. The Mennonites are one of these Germanic religious sects who settled in Ontario.

They were really good farmers. They used horses to get about, including ploughing and carriages. They would not pay taxes, but they did not accept anything from the government either. I replaced the hip on one. When he came back for a recheck, he asked me how much he owed. I did not know what to say. I certainly was not going to charge him what I charged my overseas patients, so I suggested $1,000. He pulled a roll of bills out of his pocket and counted out the money, gave it to me, and left. When I asked him about rechecks, he said if he had problems, he would get back to me. I guess everything went OK because I never heard from him again.

I liked Roland. He taught me to speak a little Delaware so we could insult other people without them knowing. Roland came to my last wedding and to my child's birthdays. He gave him a child's version of traditional dress with buckskins, headdress, and all once. Roland eventually became an elder in his band. He once brought to the hospital his full eagle feather headdress.

The third member was Jane, a Filipina. As I have mentioned before, if the nursing schools in the Philippines closed, Western medicine would have to close down. Again, what can I say? She was so clever that I would play a game with her to educate the residents. I always told them that they should know the operation well enough, that they could recite from memory the sequence of instruments they would use in the operation. Jane's husband loved to barbecue, as many Filipinos do, so a group of us would visit Jane's house a few times every summer.

All good things come to an end. I was in despair. The team had gone. But miracles happen. A nurse arrived from China. Management had actually spoken to me about this girl who had applied some time before. They were uncertain as to where she was from, somewhere they had never heard of. They knew I had been in China several times, so they asked me. They told me she was from Harbin. I knew that as being the most polluted city in the world. Its second claim to fame is the ice palace. In Quebec every year and I think in Sweden, they build an ice hotel where one can stay, eat at tables of carved ice, and sleep on an ice bed. But these only have one story. In Harbin, they make a three-story ice palace every year. If she was a nurse, she would not be politically connected. So here was a woman who was not politically connected, who escaped with her family from the worst hellhole in China (perhaps I exaggerate, but if so, not by much). I recommended they hire her immediately, and they did, and she was all I expected her to be. Julia's children ate the Canadian education system alive, ending up with full scholarships at the best engineering university.

The other two who came were Urmi from India, by way of the rest of the world as she seemed to have worked everywhere, and Irina from Russia, by way of Israel. I sometimes thought that when I was with these women, they should have been operating, and I should have been assisting them.

I had all sorts of specialized equipment that people had given me over the years. For example, I needed a high-speed burr to do some revision cases, but the equipment cost more than the hospital could afford. So I phoned Dr. Anspach in Florida, who was the developer and manufacturer. I told him I was a poor Canadian and could not afford his equipment and asked if he had any castoffs. He thought for a minute and then said that he had had a pretty good year, so he gave me $35,000 of free equipment. The generosity of some of the Americans was simply astounding. Similarly, a British surgeon developed an ultrasonic system (OSCAR) to remove cement from the inside of bones. I approached the company and offered to help sell it for them in the US if they gave me a unit, as my hospital certainly could not afford to buy it. They did, and I did. Urmi and Irena knew all about this special stuff of mine, secreted in the back storage room. If one of my colleagues needed some of my specialized equipment, I got one of these girls to scrub and show the surgeon how to use it.

Urmi just knew everything. She had a memory like mine. When I would bitch and moan, she would suggest that I go back to Aminabad with her, and we would build our own hospital. I was in Aminabad once, lecturing. In the evening, it was forty degrees, so while that was a tempting offer, I didn't think so. Some parts of India can be really hot. I was once lecturing in Mangalore, and I went for a walk on the beach to see all the freighters, which were very close inshore there. I thought I was going to melt. That evening, we had a little party in the hotel gardens. The temperature had moderated, and it was just so nice under the stars. What was even nicer was that it was close to Jhansi, and it so happened that only the professor and I knew anything about the famous Rani. It seemed that they do not teach history in India any more than they teach it in Canada.

I remember the first time Irena was going to scrub for my hip implant, which she had never seen before. She took home all the manuals in the operating room on that design, and by the next day, she knew it all and would teach the other surgeons if they had to use it. Irena knew her Russian literature, which I could never read, so she used to educate me. I remember once that I had quoted that "we all have our appointment in Samarra." We were trying to work out who had said that. She thought it sounded like Chekov and that Samarra was in Siberia. The anesthetist eventually tracked it down, and it turned out to be W. Somerset Maugham's, and Samarra is in Iraq. I fact-checked just now, and it actually was probably an American, John O'Hara.

Working with these three nurses just made life so easy and so pleasant. They were so quick and slick and were never at a loss. The only thing I did not like, which has been a constant refrain of mine, was that when my operating list was finished, they had to go and help other rooms instead of going home. As in so many things, Bombelli was right.

CHAPTER 29

SLOWING DOWN

After thirty-plus years of being a road warrior, I was beginning to slow down, but then China started to open up. I had first been there about thirty years before, and it was an utter wasteland. The difference now is hard to believe; Beijing is full of trees and cars and superb western hotels.

Most of the implants they had been using were homemade, and it showed. They were knockoffs of stuff that had been obsolete in the West for more than a decade, and one really would not like to inquire too closely what the metal actually was. I was there several times, lecturing and operating. I remember one horrendous case in Jinan, the city of Confucius, in the Shandong province. When I put the implant in, I could not reduce the hip because the tissues were so scarred from previous surgeries. I shortened the femur around a fully seated implant, which I am sure the observing surgeons had never seen before because I had never done it before, and no one had described it. The case took me so long to do that I did not have a chance to see the Yellow River flowing along like an aqueduct above ground level.

Another place I remember was with Professor Hee in the Hangzhou, which has the Great Western Lake with the Broken Bridge, which Chinese find so romantic. I once went to Suzhou because it was supposed to be the town with the most beautiful women in the world. It did not seem that way to me, but a lady judge I know in Toronto who is from Shanghai herself, which is very close, said that was because men have come from all over the world to marry these women and take them away.

There was a meeting in Beijing in April. Beijing is about as far north as Toronto, so it was still cold. There was a very good hip surgeon I knew in Beijing. She asked me to come to her hospital to consult. She had just done a case of a high congenital hip dislocation. This is a condition where the baby is born with a dislocated hip. If not taken care of immediately, the person grows up with effectively no hip joint, so the leg is very short.

When the hip is being replaced in such a case, the surgeon will make the leg longer, but very few try to equalize the leg lengths. The reason for this is that the nerve will only stretch so far. In the US, if the nerve is damaged, the surgeon is sued, so few will lengthen more than two centimeters. I have published research on this and will lengthen a lot more, if appropriate, up to seven centimeters. After all, patients like to have legs the same length.

This Beijing surgeon who was technically very skillful had done the daughter of a high Communist official. Maybe because I was in town, or maybe not, she had equalized the girl's leg lengths, in other words, lengthened the short leg considerably. If one lengthens a leg, the muscles around the hip are stretched and therefore very tight. This pulls the leg out to the side, so when the patient wakes up from the anesthetic, they feel that the leg is hugely overlong. The muscles relax after the first few days, the leg comes back to midline, and the legs are then obviously the same length. Patients were told about this before surgery, but it still came as a shock to some or most of them.

This girl was inconsolable, which was what I was doing there, trying to explain via an interpreter that everything would be just fine. Obviously, neither she nor her parents believed me.

I had been scheduled to go south to Guilin, which is almost tropical, so I was dressed for that because I was going to be in Beijing for a couple of days only. Instead, I found myself in Xinjiang, on the Silk Road, in the middle of what seemed to be the Gobi Desert. I ran a clinic for patients with severe joint problems. There were about thirty people, so with an interpreter, it took some time. This was April, and the temperature was about zero, and they had the windows open.

By the time I had finished the clinic, I had severe hypothermia and could not stop shivering. I told them they had to take me somewhere warm, so they took me to the operating room. It was about thirty-eight degrees with about 100 percent humidity, so my glasses steamed up, so I had to have them taken off. There were three professors scrubbed to assist me. The Shanghai doctor who was supposed to translate for me was so overawed he could not speak, so I had to speak to the scrub nurse in gorilla manner, which consisted of grunts and pointing.

What was even worse was, they had brought knee replacement instruments I had never seen before. All in all, it was what the Americans would say, a SNAFU, and I was scheduled to do a bilateral total knee replacement. So I did it by eye. I mean, I can do it with no instruments, as after all, I have done over five thousand knee replacements. The problem is, I cannot explain to anyone else how to do it without instruments. I cannot readily explain how you stick your thumbs in and feel the pressure and release until the pressure is the same. Equally, it is difficult to explain, even if they speak English, that the landmarks to cut with the power saw are the floor, the corner of the room, and the anesthetist sitting at the head of the table. I mean, do a couple of hundred knees, and then we can maybe talk.

The other problem is that if I am operating by eye only, the operation moves along quite smartly, as after all, I do not have to stop and measure things, so it takes about ten minutes to put the components in. It still takes about twenty minutes to sew up. So I am not sure how much benefit that show-and-tell operation was to anyone except the patient.

Actually, it is not good to have the professor scrubbed during a show-and-tell operation. He always tends to invite the professors from the surrounding hospitals or towns to scrub also. It was like that in Milan once. Gianni, who was a great surgeon himself, as everyone knows, had invited two additional colleagues when I was doing a hip exchange. Everyone was helping, which is not good. Once the femur broke, there was a certain lack of interest, but fortunately, the artificial hip I was demonstrating could handle fractured femurs, so the operation ended up being a better demonstration than I had planned.

From Xinjiang, I made it back home, but I never saw the Beijing surgeon again. Before that, I would meet her occasionally in the US or Korea. Where she went or was sent, I do not know. I am afraid that "they have taken my beloved with the pack horses to the north. The chains are set on the feet that were set on my heart."

I should not say that as she was a happily married woman, but I could not resist. I have been waiting to use that quotation for years.

After the Twin Towers, travel became so difficult that obviously the terrorists won their objective. Lineups for security became a nightmare, especially inside the US. Japan alone seemed to have escaped the mania of searching elderly nuns for bombs. The Traveling Road Show slowly ground down, as no one wanted to undertake the misery of frequent flying. Many of the men involved retired or moved out of the big hospitals into small community hospitals or simply sent their junior colleagues to do the lecturing. The juniors did not object very much, as after all, if all you have ever known is misery, you think that that is normal.

CHAPTER 30

PROBLEMS

The technology of joint replacement surgery has really not changed in the last ten years. There are several reasons for this. Perhaps the results are so good that it is hard to improve them. But I don't know if that is true. People can forget which hip has been done, but no one forgets which knee. This means they are feeling something. The forgettable knee therefore should be the ultimate goal.

There are problems with that. Patients who have no sensation in their joints abuse them so badly that they overstress them, and their own joints fall apart. There actually is a condition called congenital absence of pain, and these people become crippled in childhood as they destroy their joints. The same thing happens to the fingers of lepers who have no sensation. Artificial joints have no sensation, so in theory, people can damage an artificial joint without knowing it. In fact, most feel something, although they cannot tell what it is. I think that they are either feeling the surrounding scar tissue, which has some sensation, or more likely, they are feeling the strain on the attachment of the joint to the bone.

Any bearing has a finite life expectancy, but as humans also have a finite life expectancy, that should be a problem that could be solved. Similarly, fixation of the implant we really solved in the '70s, although there are still some minor issues, but that is only because no one has been interested in them. These are technical problems, and they can be solved if there is ever any will to do so. Better materials are possible, and putting sensors into the materials is not an outlandish concept.

The immediate problems are more sociological than physical. In writing this book, I was struck how often I used the phrase "this would not be possible nowadays."

The dead hand of the government kills all innovation. One can see this in bodies like the FDA, which have made it prohibitively expensive to develop new drugs. Companies can make much more profit out of a simple "me too," and even when they come up with a new drug, some governments essentially steal it by ignoring patents and producing so-called generics. The joint replacement field is not quite as bad, but it is certainly going the same way. Some countries now will not allow any new product into their state-run system.

Engineering is not philosophy, and it costs real money to turn theory into practice. I suppose it could be argued that we have gone far enough, and this certainly seems to be the consensus among the political classes. This can be seen in any technology the government thinks it understands. That pitiful little tin can masquerading as a space station is a good example.

Similarly, university research is coming to a grinding halt as everything is overseen by review boards, which largely consist of a few who long since gave up research or the many who never did any at all, ever. When I started, a research grant went to the researcher. Now a minimum of 30 percent goes to the institution, whether they are involved or not. Someone, after all, has to pay for the endlessly reproducing administration. They naturally look on new ideas with suspicion, as there may have been nothing published on it. What they prefer is a "me too" research project on something wherein there are already hundreds of publications all saying the same thing. *New* is frightening and dangerous.

Patient perception is now also changing. Everything is expected to work 100 percent of the time, produce no symptoms at all, and last forever. Maybe someday!

Another problem is back pain. The disks in the human back begin to fail at age twenty and worsen with age. We still have no useful human artificial disks. As I found out almost forty years ago, no company currently outside the medical field wants to get involved. The lessons of the Dow Corning junk-science disaster have not gone away, and this is reinforced every day by those who would ban fluoride in water and the anti-immunization brigade.

All we can realistically do for painful disks is fuse them, which means stop the movement. If one does this then, while the pain from that level goes away, the movement is forced to occur above and below the fused segment, and those disks wear out. Forty years ago, we thought that that was a pretty good operation. What we were looking for then was a better way of fusing disks. I was working with bone-growth stimulation, but others were trying different methods. I still remember Art Steffee from Cleveland coming to Toronto to show Ian Macnab his new idea. I knew Art, and I knew Dr. Macnab, so Art flew up to see me, and I took him along to introduce him. At that time, Dr. Macnab was one of the best-known spine surgeons in the world.

Art had developed a technique of stabilizing the spine with metal plates and screws. It looked terrifyingly dangerous, but he had worked out how to do it. Dr. Macnab looked at his plans and his data and said that he thought it would work. That was all Art needed to hear. It was a little embarrassing to be walking down the street with a very large middle-aged man skipping beside you, like a happy child. Art revolutionized spine fusion surgery, but it had not improved that much since then.

The relevance of this to joint replacement surgery is that spine pain can radiate down the leg, and so patients may think that they have a bad hip or knee when it is really their back.

The training of surgeons is now different. Robert Judet, the great French surgeon, used to laugh at me and think that the volume of surgery I had done was pitiful. But at least I could, at one time, do everything. Now the joint replacement surgeons really have not done much spine, so all they have is a hammer, and if all you have is a hammer, everything is a nail. Replacing someone's knee or hip is not really going to help their back pain.

There is also the princess and the pea syndrome. The way one can tell a European princess from a commoner is that when she sleeps on a bed, she can feel a pea on the bed under seven mattresses. Discomfort is no longer to be tolerated, so minor degree of arthritis ends up getting an artificial joint. Unfortunately, if there was not actually much pain to begin with, as opposed to perceived pain, surgery will not help much, and the disappointment will be overwhelming.

CHAPTER 31

REQUIEM

Think, in this batter'd caravanserai
Whose portals are alternate night and day
How sultan after sultan with his pomp
Abode his destined hour and went his way

I still miss getting out of the hospital in late afternoons into the limo to fly off to the places of my youth and dreams. I miss the people with whom I fought, like the great Heinz Wagner, long since gone to rest. I miss the road warriors with whom I drank, laughed, boasted, and lied. I remember the people without whose help none of this journey would have been possible: Ian Macnab, Bob Pilliar, Isobel Urquhart, and Jerry Kent, and all the wonderful nurses I had the privilege of working with.

But we don't get out of this one alive. I got very sick but recovered. As a patient told me once, "If you are this side of the grass, you are having a good day."

It seems a fair philosophy. So tempus fugit, but someday I want to go back for sakura time and sit and dream.

They say the lion and lizard keep
The courts where Jamshid gloried and drank deep
And Bahram, that great hunter—the wild ass
Stamps o'er his head as he lies fast asleep.

Or the other great one,
They are not long, the days of wine and roses:
Out of a misty dream
Our path emerges for a while, then closes
Within a dream.

CPSIA information can be obtained
at www.ICGtesting.com
Printed in the USA
LVHW092145130919
631048LV00002B/2/P